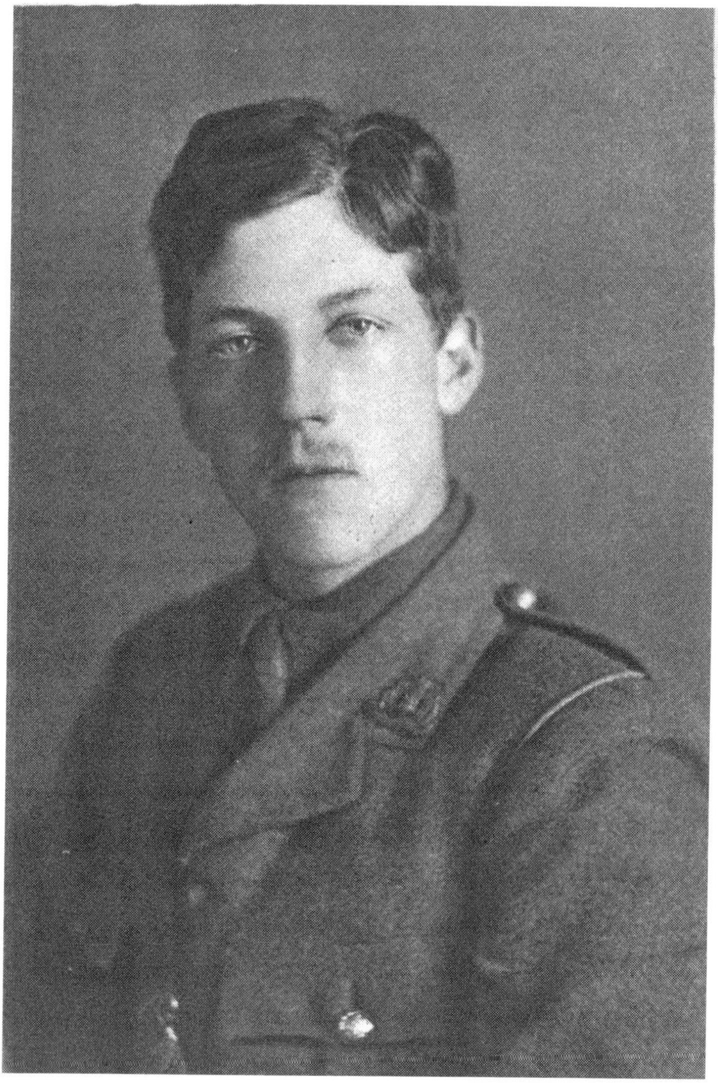

DEATH AND THE DOWNS:
THE POETRY OF
CHARLES HAMILTON SORLEY

Edited and annotated by
BRETT RUTHERFORD

YOGH & THORN BOOKS
PROVIDENCE, RI

Yogh & Thorn Edition August 2010

Originally Published as Marlborough and Other Poems, *January 1916*
Second Edition, slightly enlarged, February 1916
Reprinted, February, April, May 1916
Third Edition, with "Illustrations in Prose," November 1916
Fourth Edition, re-arranged and re-set, May 1919
Fifth Edition, 1922
'Miscellany' Edition, 1932

The poetry of Charles Hamilton Sorley (1895-1915)
is in the Public Domain.
Notes and Annotations Copyright 2010 by Brett Rutherford.
This book incorporates additional material from
The Letters of Charles Sorley *(1919) and*
The Soldier Poets *(1919).*
C.H.S.: An Annotated Checklist *included*
with permission of Larry Uffelman.

Yogh & Thorn Books are published by
THE POET'S PRESS
279-½ Thayer Street/ Providence, RI 02906
www.poetspress.org

ISBN 0-922558-47-7 (paperback)
ISBN 0-922558-46-9 (hardcover)

CONTENTS

Preface to the Fifth Edition, 1932   vii
Editor's Note, 2010   x

OF THE DOWNS

I	Barbury Camp	3
II	Stones	6
III	East Kennet Church at Evening	9
IV	Autumn Dawn	11
V	Return	15
VI	Richard Jefferies	16
VII	J. B.	19
VIII	The Other Wise Man	21
IX	Marlborough	26
X	Le Revenant	29
XI	Lost	32

OF SCHOOL

XII	Rain	35
XIII	A Tale of Two Careers	38
XIV	What You Will	42

OF LIFE AND THOUGHT

XV	A Call to Action	47
XVI	Peace	50
XVII	The River	52
XVIII	The Seekers	55
XIX	Rooks	57
XX	Rooks (II)	59
XXI	The Song of the Ungirt Runners	61
XXII	German Rain	62
XXIII	Brand	63
XXIV	Peer Gynt	64
XXV	To Poets	65
XXVI	"If I Have Suffered Pain"	66
XXVII	Whom Therefore We Ignorantly Worship	68
XXVIII	Deus Loquitor	69
XXIX	Expectans Expectavi	70

OF WAR AND DEATH

XXX	"All the Hills and Vales Along"	73
XXXI	To Germany	75
XXXII	"A Hundred Thousand Million Mites We Go"	76
XXXIII	Two Sonnets	77
XXXIV	"When You See Millions of the Mouthless Dead"	79
XXXV	"There is Such Change In All Those Fields"	80
XXXVI	"I Have Not Brought My *Odyssey*"	82
XXXVII	In Memoriam S.C.W., V.C.	86
XXXVIII	Behind the Lines	87

ILLUSTRATIONS IN PROSE

I	Richard Jefferies	93
II	Ibsen	95
III	The Odyssey	98
IV	Germany	102
V	Many a Better One	109
VI	"Blank Summer's Surfeit"	110
VII	"Eternally to Do"	111
VIII	"The Grandeur of Their Mess"	115
IX	"The Old War-Joy, the Old War-Pain"	116
X	"Perhaps the Road Up Ilsley Way"	119
XI	Sorley As Translator	122

CRITICISM AND SORLEIANA

C.H.S.: An Annotated Checklist
   Larry Uffelman   125
Prometheus Vinctus Loquitur (CHS)   146
Biographical Note
   Janetta Smith Sorley   146
Sorley in Training (CHS, Letter)   157
Concerning Rupert Brooke
   (CHS, Letter)   158
Charles Sorley at the Front   160
His Last Letter (CHS)   162
Bibliography   163
About This Book   165

PREFACE TO THE FIFTH EDITION, 1932

The call for a new edition of these poems gives an opportunity for issuing them in a form which is intended to be definitive.

They are now arranged in four groups according to subject. It is true that all of them perhaps might be described by the title of one of these groups, as poems of life and thought. But some owe their inspiration directly to nature — to the wind-swept downs which the author loved and which he looked upon as "wise" as well as "wide"; a few reflect the experiences of school life; yet others show how his spirit faced the great adventure of war and death. Within each group the poems are printed, as nearly as may be, in the order of their composition, the title-poem being restored to its proper chronological place. When the date, exact or approximate, is known, it has been given; in those cases in which the date specifies the day of the month, it has been taken from the author's manuscript.

A single piece of imaginative prose is included amongst the poems. Other passages of prose were added to the third edition with the view of illustrating ideas occurring in the poems and prominent in the author's mind. With the exception of a few sentences from an early essay, these prose passages are all taken from familiar letters. To the present edition a few notes have been appended, in which some topical allusions are explained and what is known about the origin of the separate pieces is told.

* * *

Of the author personally, and of what he was to his family and his friends, I do not speak. Yet I may quote the phrase used by a German lady in whose house he had been living for three months. "The time with him," she wrote, "was like a holiday and a feast-day." Many have felt what she put into words: though it was the graver moods of his mind that, for the most part, sought expression in his poems.

I may also put on record here the main facts concerning his short life.

He was born at Old Aberdeen on 19th May 1895. His father was then a professor in the University of Aberdeen, and he was of Scottish descent on both sides.

From 1900 onwards his home was in Cambridge. He was educated at Marlborough College, which he entered in September 1908 and left in December 1913, after obtaining a scholarship at University College, Oxford.

Owing to the war he never went into residence at the University. After leaving school he spent a little more than six months in Germany, first at Schwerin in Mecklenburg and afterwards, for the summer session, at the University of Jena. He was on a walking tour on the banks of the Moselle when the European war broke out. He was put in prison at Trier on the 2nd August, but released the same night with orders to leave the country.

After some adventures he reached home on the 6th, and at once applied for a commission in the army. He was gazetted Second Lieutenant in the Seventh (Service) Battalion of the Suffolk Regiment before the end of the month, Lieutenant in November, and Captain in the following August.

He was sent to France with his battalion on 30th May 1915, and served for some months in the trenches round Ploegsteert. Shortly after he had entered upon his life there, a suggestion was made to him about printing a slim volume of verse. But he put the suggestion aside as premature. "Besides," he added, "this is no time for oliveyards and vineyards, more especially of the small-holdings type. For three years or the duration of the war, let be."

Four months later his warfare was accomplished. His battalion was moved south to take part in the battle of Loos, and he fell on 13th October 1915, in an attack in which the "hair-pin" trench near Hulluch was captured by his company. "Being made perfect in a little while, he fulfilled long years."

—W. R. Sorley
Cambridge, March 1919

The Fifth Edition is an exact reprint of the Fourth Edition except for a few verbal changes [in "Rooks II" and "German Rain"]. These changes are due to the recovery, after nearly six years, of some of the author's manuscripts which he had left behind him in Germany in August 1914. —W. R. S.

EDITOR'S NOTE, 2010

Robert Graves was close enough to the Battle of Loos to hear the guns in the distance. He was briefly called to join in reinforcements for the battle. In his autobiography, Graves writes: "Gradually the noise died down, and at last a message came from Brigade that we would not be needed. It had been another dud show, chiefly notorious for the death of Charles Sorley, a twenty-year-old captain in the Suffolks, one of three poets of importance killed during the war. (The other two were Isaac Rosenberg and Wilfred Owen)."[1]

Sorley's work has survived principally in World War I anthologies, and there solely, and necessarily, with those poems concerned with the war. Sorley's "Song of the Ungirt Runners" also comes to light occasionally and is a perennial schoolboy favorite in Britain.

Sorley died at twenty, and his publication career spanned only two years. His posthumous book of poems — ranging from the earliest published school poems to the poem found in his kit after the Battle of Loos — went through a number of editions through 1932. The book appears to have been out of print since the mid-1970s. This edition attempts to redress that wrong, and to introduce Sorley's wonderful poetry to a new generation of students, fellow poets, and general readers.

For the present edition, the order of Sorley's poems has been retained as originally published in the five successive editions of *Marlborough and Other Poems*. The original end-notes written by W.R. Sorley, the poet's father, have been repositioned in this volume as footnotes with Mr. Sorley's initials, interspersed with my own new notes and annotations.

The passing of time, and today's disinclination toward the classics, suggested that a number of new annotations on classical and Biblical allusions, persons, place names, and historical events, were in order. Since so few readers

---

[1] Robert Graves, *Good-Bye to All That*, p. 169

today can read Greek, I have transliterated Sorley's Greek references into the Latin alphabet so that the casual reader can get a sense of the compressed power and sensual beauty of that language; the Greek and German footnote translations are by Sorley's father.

With the student reader in mind, I have provided additional footnotes elaborating Homeric references, and I have translated Latin titles and phrases where appropriate. Sorley's allusions to Biblical titles in Latin, and to familiar phrases from hymns and sermons, would have been recognized by his contemporaries, but for many of us today, this counts as a lost discourse; I have annotated those references that came to my attention, but I am sure I have missed some. (As a heathen youth I was spared the indoctrination of catechisms and hymns).

During his poetic youth, Pindar was once attacked for excessive mythological allusions by fellow poet Corinna, who advised him: "Sow with the hand, not with the whole sack." I hazard the same criticism in annotating Sorley. My desire everywhere is to make these poems more self-explicating by providing the necessary context. A great part of the poignancy of Sorley's poetry, and his tragically brief life, comes from knowing that this young man, fluent in Greek and Latin and well on his way to mastering German, lived with one foot in the ancient world even as he sat in the trenches. Although Sorley complains "I have not brought my *Odyssey*," the "old windy walls of Troy" are as real to him as the next hill in the battlefield.

I am grateful to Jane Berard, who wrote about Wiltshire and its hill-forts, and who kindly made available some items from her library that helped me visualize the haunted landscape of Sorley's youth. Thanks are due also to John Trause, for glancing over my rusty Latin and stumbling Greek translations/transliterations. (On his counsel I have adopted the Library of Congress transliteration system for Greek.)

From a 1903 edition of Richard Jefferies, I have extracted Clifton Johnson's photographs of the landscape both Jefferies and Sorley loved. These glimpses of the pre-war countryside may help readers appreciate Sorley's nature-worship connected with the Wiltshire landscape.

The "Illustrations in Prose" were selected by Sorley *père* from the poet's letters, arranged according to the background information they shed on particular poems in the book. Since these notes are too long to be re-deployed as footnotes, I have retained this section along with the reference to specific poems. I have annotated this section extensively for the benefit of today's reader, and I will welcome communication from scholars who might possess additional information about Sorley's readings and travels. The "Illustrations" reveal Sorley not only as a classicist, but also as an avid reader of English poetry right up to his own era. His attitudes toward Germany and the war reveal a mind already seasoned with cool rationality, wiser in many ways than the elders who hurled him into battle. At the same time, his opinions on war, death and religion mark him as a true poetic "outsider." His silence on romantic love of any kind, outside of comparing Helen of Troy with a German Frau, can be attributed to extreme youth and the intervention of a sniper's bullet.

From the 1919 *Letters of Charles Sorley*, I learned that Charles Sorley had a twin brother, a fact not mentioned in any edition of *Marlborough and Other Poems*. I have included the biographical chapter about the poet written by his mother, in which Kenneth William, his twin, is mentioned but not named. I added proper names and other details to Mrs. Sorley's text in square brackets.

Sorley's fascination with Ibsen's twin-drama *John Gabriel Borkman* takes on a new light when one knows that he himself was a twin. Further, Sorley's fascination with Helen of Troy becomes psychologically more complex considering the myth of the phantom twin "Egyptian Helen" and the manufactured Helen-twin at the center of Act III of Goethe's *Faust II*

From the *Letters*, I have also chosen several additional texts that shed light on Sorley's attitudes toward the war (a letter to a school friend that would not have been publishable anytime during the war); his response to the death of fellow-poet Rupert Brooke; an account of his combat experience in the trenches by a fellow soldier; and his final letter home.

Another welcome addition to this book came from Prof. Larry Uffelman, who consented to a reprint of most of his annotated checklist tracking the reception of Sorley's work from 1915 through 1974. The literature regarding Sorley has been sparse since then, especially with his complete poetry, his letters, and the biography by Thomas Burnett Swan long unavailable. Although we now have a new, postmodern perspective on this era's poetry, and many new critical lenses through which to view it, Swann's 1965 assessment of critical disinterest in Sorley is still pertinent:

> He was never a member of a group or clique of poets. He was not an Imagist, with an Ezra Pound or an Amy Lowell to trumpet his fame and keep him before the public. Though he wrote in the era of the Georgian poets, he was never one of them; he did not appear in their famous anthologies, and unlike Brooke and James Elroy Flecker he had no Edward Marsh to guide his career. Later, in the Twenties and Thirties, his traditional forms could hardly appeal to members of the Eliot-Pound tradition, with their love for experiment, and today his staunch, even though unconventional, religion and austere principles are not calculated to attract the Beatniks...[2]

"Death and the Downs" was the poet's working title for poem xxxiii. I chose this title for the entire book, since Sorley's last work, and the circumstances of his death, form the most compelling aspect of our continued interest in him. This also avoids employing a title that American readers would, alas, associate with a brand of cigarettes. The new title encompasses both Sorley as war poet and Sorley as nature-rhapsodist.

Brett Rutherford
University of Rhode Island
September 19, 2010

---

[2] Swan, Thomas Burnett. *The Ungirt Runner: Charles Hamilton Sorley, Poet of World War I.* p. 131

P.S. In 1985, Sorley's name was inscribed on a memorial stone for World War I poets at the Poets' Corner in Westminster Abbey.

With characteristic British reticence, Sorley's father made no mention of where his son is buried. There is no marked grave for the poet. The military cemetery at Loos has a long wall, the "Memorial to the Missing" where Sorley's name — one of the "pale battalion" of some 20,000 soldiers killed — is inscribed. His kit, including the penciled manuscript of "When you see millions of the mouthless dead," is all that came home.

OF THE DOWNS[1]

---

[1] *Downs*. Old English word referring to hills, but more specifically, the hill-forts such as those that dot the Wiltshire landscape. The term "downs" is seldom used in the United States, and its counterintuitive meaning here prompts a cross-Atlantic footnote. —BR

I
BARBURY CAMP[2]

We burrowed night and day with tools of lead,[3]
Heaped the bank up and cast it in a ring
And hurled the earth above. And Caesar said,
"Why, it is excellent. I like the thing."
We, who are dead,
Made it, and wrought, and Caesar liked the thing.[4]

And here we strove, and here we felt each vein
Ice-bound, each limb fast-frozen, all night long.
And here we held communion with the rain
That lashed us into manhood with its thong,
Cleansing through pain.
And the wind visited us and made us strong.

---

[2] Barbury Camp is on the northern escarpment of the Marlborough downs, between five and six miles north by west from Marlborough. The camp on the summit is of pre-Roman origin. The preference for rain and windy weather, shown in this and other poems in the book, has suggested the poem entitled "Sorley's Weather" by Capt. Robert Graves *(Fairies and Fusiliers,* 1917) which ends with the verse,
"Yet rest there, Shelley, on the sill, / For though the winds come frorely/ I'm away to the rain-blown hill / And the ghost of Sorley." —WRS.
[3] The Romans mined lead in Northumberland and Somerset later in their occupation, but lead is too soft a metal for use as tools. Perhaps Sorley could not find rhymes for "bronze" or "iron," the more likely materials. —BR
[4] *Caesar*. Roman general Julius Caesar invaded Britain in 55 and 54 BCE; the Emperor Claudius "reconquered" Britain for Rome in 43 CE; and the emperor Hadrian pushed the frontier further northward into Scotland in 122 CE. Parts of Britain remained under Roman rule until 410 CE. In Sorley's time, many of the hill-forts were assumed to be Roman ruins, when in fact the Romans occupied and built over hill-forts dating from the Iron Age. Indeed, this has been called "the most impressive Neolithic landscape in the country" (Coones & Patten 94). — BR

Up from around us, numbers without name,
Strong men and naked, vast, on either hand
Pressing us in, they came. And the wind came
And bitter rain, turning grey all the land.
That was our game,
To fight with men and storms, and it was grand.

For many days we fought them, and our sweat
Watered the grass, making it spring up green,
Blooming for us. And, if the wind was wet,
Our blood wetted the wind, making it keen
With the hatred
And wrath and courage that our blood had been.

So, fighting men and winds and tempests, hot
With joy and hate and battle-lust, we fell
Where we fought. And God said,
    "Killed at last then? What!
Ye that are too strong for heaven, too clean for hell,
(God said) stir not.
This be your heaven, or, if ye will, your hell."

So again we fight and wrestle, and again
Hurl the earth up and cast it in a ring.
But when the wind comes up, driving the rain
(Each rain-drop a fiery steed), and the mists rolling
Up from the plain,
This wild procession, this impetuous thing,

Hold us amazed. We mount the wind-cars, then
Whip up the steeds and drive through all the world,
Searching to find somewhere some brethren,
Sons of the winds and waters of the world.
We, who were men,
Have sought, and found no men in all this world.

Wind, that has blown here always ceaselessly,
Bringing, if any man can understand,
Might to the mighty, freedom to the free;
Wind, that has caught us, cleansed us, made us grand,
Wind that is we
(We that were men) — make men in all this land,

That so may live and wrestle and hate that when
They fall at last exultant, as we fell,
And come to God, God may say, "Do you come then
Mildly enquiring, is it heaven or hell?
Why! Ye were men!
Back to your winds and rains. Be these your heaven
 and hell!"

24 March 1913

II
STONES[5]

This field is almost white with stones
    That cumber all its thirsty crust.
And underneath, I know, are bones,
    And all around is death and dust.

And if you love a livelier hue —
    O, if you love the youth of year,
When all is clean and green and new,
    Depart. There is no summer here.

Albeit, to me there lingers yet
    In this forbidding stony dress
The impotent and dim regret
    For some forgotten restlessness.

Dumb, imperceptibly astir,
    These relics of an ancient race,
These men, in whom the dead bones were
    Still fortifying their resting-place.

Their field of life was white with stones;
    Good fruit to earth they never brought.
O, in these bleached and buried bones
    Was neither love nor faith nor thought.

---

[5] Printed in *The Marlburian*, 28 July 1913. In this case, and in a few other cases, the text in the book varies slightly from that given in *The Marlburian*, In these variations the author's manuscript has been followed. —WRS

But like the wind in this bleak place,
    Bitter and bleak and sharp they grew,
And bitterly they ran their race,
    A brutal, bad, unkindly crew:

Souls like the dry earth, hearts like stone,
    Brains like that barren bramble-tree:
Stern, sterile, senseless, mute, unknown —
    But bold, O, bolder far than we !

14 July 1913

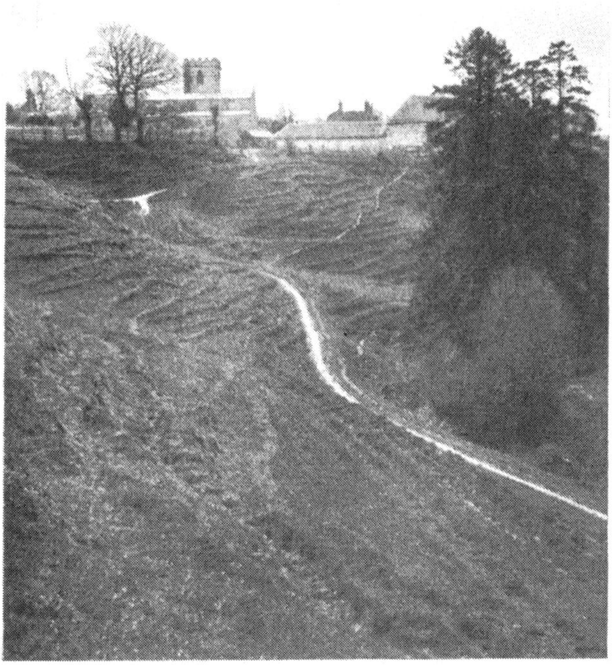

III
EAST KENNET CHURCH AT EVENING[6]

I stood amongst the corn, and watched
    The evening coming down.
The rising vale was like a queen,
    And the dim church her crown.

Crown-like it stood against the hills.
    Its form was passing fair.
I almost saw the tribes go up
    To offer incense there.

And far below the long vale stretched.
    As a sleeper she did seem
That after some brief restlessness
    Has now begun to dream.

(All day the wakefulness of men,
    Their lives and labours brief,
Have broken her long troubled sleep.
    Now, evening brings relief.)

There was no motion there, nor sound.
    She did not seem to rise.
Yet was she wrapping herself in
    Her grey of night-disguise.

---

[6] Published in *The Marlburian*, 3 December 1913. East Kennet is a village on the Kennet between four and five miles west of Marlborough. A correspondent, who is familiar with the district, thinks that the church seen by the author from the cornfield was not that of East Kennet but the neighbouring church of West Overton. —WRS

For now no church nor tree nor fold
    Was visible to me:
Only that fading into one
    Which God must sometimes see.

No coloured glory streaked the sky
    To mark the sinking sun.
There was no redness in the west
    To tell that day was done.

Only, the greyness of the eve
    Grew fuller than before.
And, in its fulness, it made one
    Of what had once been more.

There was much beauty in that sight
    That man must not long see.
God dropped the kindly veil of night
    Between its end and me.

24 July 1913

IV
AUTUMN DAWN[7]

And this is morning. Would you think
That this was the morning, when the land
Is full of heavy eyes that blink
Half-opened, and the tall trees stand
Too tired to shake away the drops
Of passing night that cling around
Their branches and weigh down their tops:
And the grey sky leans on the ground?
The thrush sings once or twice, but stops
Affrighted by the silent sound.
The sheep, scarce moving, munches, moans.
The slow herd mumbles, thick with phlegm.
The grey road-mender, hacking stones,
Is now become as one of them.
Old mother Earth has rubbed her eyes
And stayed, so senseless, lying down.
Old mother is too tired to rise
And lay aside her grey nightgown,
And come with singing and with strength
In loud exuberance of day,
Swift-darting. She is tired at length,
Done up, past bearing, you would say.
She'll come no more in lust of strife,
In hedge's leap, and wild bird's cries,[8]
In winds that cut you like a knife,

---

[7] Published in *The Marlburian,* 9 October 1913. This poem, said the author, in sending a copy of it home from Germany, "has too much copy from Meredith in it, but I value it as being (with 'Return') a memorial of my walk to Marlborough last September" (1913). The scenery of this walk is recalled in XXXVI ("I have not brought my *Odyssey*"). —WRS

[8] *hedge's, bird's;* the apostrophe was misplaced in editions 1 to 3. —WRS

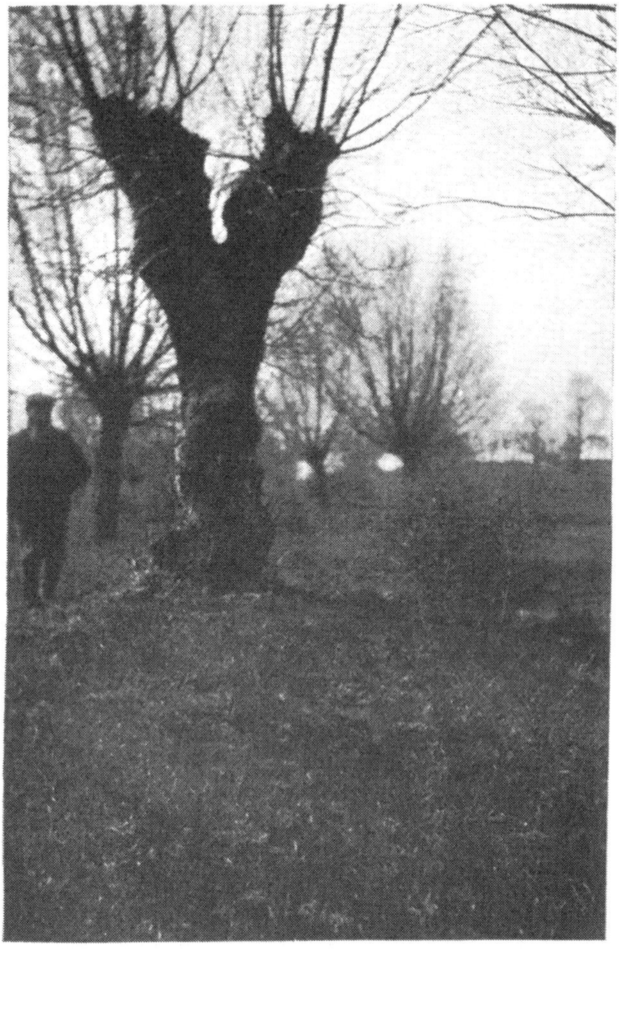

In days of laughter and swift skies,
That palpably pulsate with life,
With life that kills, with life that dies.
But in a morning such as this
Is neither life nor death to see,
Only that state which some call bliss,
Grey hopeless immortality.
Earth is at length bedrid[9]. She is
Supinest of the things that be:
And stilly, heavy with long years,
Brings forth such days in dumb regret,
Immortal days, that rise in tears,
And cannot, though they strive to, set.

* * *

The mists do move. The wind takes breath.
The sun appeareth over there,
And with red fingers hasteneth
From Earth's grey bed the clothes to tear,
And strike the heavy mist's dank tent.
And Earth uprises with a sigh.
She is astir. She is not spent.
And yet she lives and yet can die.
The grey road-mender from the ditch
Looks up. He has not looked before.
The stunted tree sways like the witch
It was: 'tis living witch once more.
The winds are washen. In the deep
Dew of the morn they've washed. The skies
Are changing dress. The clumsy sheep
Bound, and earth's many bosoms rise,

---

[9] *bedrid*. Variant of bedridden, also meaning "worn out, decrepit, impotent" (OED). —BR

And earth's green tresses spring and leap
About her brow. The earth has eyes,
The earth has voice, the earth has breath,
As o'er the land and through the air,
With wingèd sandals, Life and Death
Speed hand in hand — that winsome pair!

16 September 1913

V
RETURN

Still stand the downs so wise and wide?
    Still shake the trees their tresses grey?
I thought their beauty might have died
    Since I had been away.

I might have known the things I love,
    The winds, the flocking birds' full cry,
The trees that toss, the downs that move,
    Were longer things than I.

Lo, earth that bows before the wind,
    With wild green children overgrown,
And all her bosoms, many-whinned,[10]
    Receive me as their own.

The birds are hushed and fled: the cows
    Have ceased at last to make long moan.
They only think to browse and browse
    Until the night is grown.

The wind is stiller than it was,
    And dumbness holds the closing day.
The earth says not a word, because
    It has no word to say.

The dear soft grasses under foot
    Are silent to the listening ear.
Yet beauty never can be mute,
    And some will always hear.

18 September 1913

---

[10] *whinned*. Covered with the prickly evergreen shrub (*Ulex europaeus*) known as furze or gorse. Also called whin-bush, the plant is common throughout Northern Europe, and has been used for both fencing and fuel. —BR

VI
RICHARD JEFFERIES[11]

(LIDDINGTON CASTLE)

I see the vision of the Vale
   Rise teeming to the rampart Down,
The fields and, far below, the pale
   Red-rootedness of Swindon town.

But though I see all things remote,
   I cannot see them with the eyes
With which ere now the man from Coate[12]
   Looked down and wondered and was wise.

He knew the healing balm of night,
   The strong and sweeping joy of day,
The sensible and dear delight
   Of life, the pity of decay.

---

[11] Published in *The Marlburian,* 9 October 1913. This poem is a result of the same walk as IV and V. Liddington Castle is about seven miles north by east from Marlborough and, like Barbury Camp, guards the northern frontier of the downs. Describing a walk three months before, the author wrote, "I then scaled Liddington Castle, which is no more a castle than I am, but a big hill with a fine Roman camp on the top, and a view all down the Vale of the White Horse to the north and the Kennet valley to the south. I sat there for about an hour, reading *Wild Life in a Southern County,* with which I had come armed — the most appropriate place in the world to read it from, as it was on Liddington Castle that Richard Jefferies wrote it and many others of his books, and as it is Jefferies' description of how he saw the country from there." —WRS

[Richard Jefferies (1848-1897) is a beloved British nature writer. His keen observation of English flora and fauna, and his intense nature mysticism, make him the English equivalent to America's Thoreau. Sorley may have owned the 1881 "new" edition of *Wild Life in a Southern County,* published by Smith, Elder & Co. Jefferies begins his book by describing the view from atop the hill-fort called Liddington Castle. The "Roman earthworks" are now understood to predate the Romans, perhaps as far back as 800 BCE. The Romans simply occupied and built over a strategic Iron Age hill-fort. —BR]

[12] *Coate,* a village to the south (now a suburb) of Swindon, and the birthplace of Jefferies. —WRS

And many wondrous words he wrote,
    And something good to man he showed,
About the entering in of Coate,
    There, on the dusty Swindon road.

19 September 1913

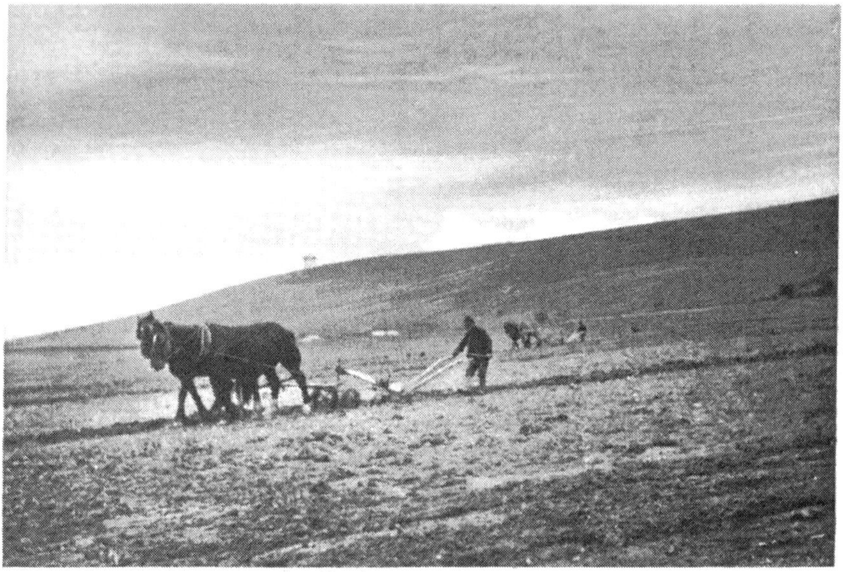

VII
J. B.[13]

There's still a horse on Granham hill[14],
And still the Kennet moves, and still
Four Miler[15] sways and is not still.
   But where is her interpreter?

The downs are blown into dismay,
The stunted trees seem all astray,
Looking for someone clad in grey
   And carrying a golf-club thing;

Who, them when he had lived among,
Gave them what they desired, a tongue.
Their words he gave them to be sung
   Perhaps were few, but they were true.

The trees, the downs, on either hand,
Still stand, as he said they would stand.
But look, the rain in all the land
   Makes all things dim with tears of him.

---

[13] *The Marlburian,* 9 October 1913. This poem is a lament over the departure of a Marlborough master, John Bain, the laureate of the school, who had resigned and left Marlborough at the end of the previous summer term. The author's acquaintance with him was entirely an out-of-school one. See note on XXXVI—WRS

[14] *Granham hill,* on the opposite side of the Kennet from Marlborough College. The *horse* is a rather inferior specimen of the "white horses," cut out in the chalk, of which there are other and more famous examples in the Wiltshire and Berkshire downs. It was cut by boys of a local proprietary school in 1804. —WRS [The famous White Horse at Uffington fort, a man-made design comprised of chalk on a hillside, is believed to be over 2,000 years old (Jenkins 166) — BR]

[15] *Four Miler,* the school name for Four Mile Clump, so-called because it lies at the fourth milestone on the old Swindon Road; it is in the same direction as Barbury Camp and about a mile short of it.—WRS [A *clump* is a cluster of trees. Four Mile Clump still stands, and bicyclists and hikers know it just as hikers did in Sorley's day. The marking stone was destroyed by a tank during military maneuvers in 1948, but the Five-Mile stone was protected, and Sorley's initials were carved onto it. —BR]

And recently the Kennet croons,
And winds are playing widowed tunes.
 — He has not left our "toun o' touns,"[16]
   But taken it away with him!

October 1913

---

[16] *toun o' touns,* one of several echoes in the poem of John Bain's school songs "The Scotch Marlburian" and "All Aboard."—WRS

VIII
THE OTHER WISE MAN[17]

(SCENE: A valley with a wood on one side and a road running up to a distant hill: as it might be, the valley to the east of West Woods[18], that runs up to Oare Hill,[19] only much larger. TIME: Autumn. Four wise men are marching hillward along the road.)

ONE WISE MAN
I wonder where the valley ends?
On, comrades, on.

ANOTHER WISE MAN
The rain-red road,
Still shining sinuously, bends
Leagues upwards.

A THIRD WISE MAN
   To the hill, O friends,
To seek the star that once has glowed
Before us; turning not to right
Nor left, nor backward once looking.
Till we have clomb[20] — and with the night
We see the King.

ALL THE WISE MEN
              The King! The King!

THE THIRD WISE MAN
Long is the road but —

---

[17] Published in *The Marlburian,* 10 February 1914. —WRS
[18] West Woods are on the western side of the valley and nearer Marlborough. —WRS
[19] Oare Hill is on the north-eastern border of Pewsey Vale between three and four miles from Marlborough College. West Woods are on the western side of the valley and nearer Marlborough. —WRS
[20] *Clomb.* Archaic variant of climbed. —BR

A FOURTH WISE MAN
        Brother, see,
There, to the left, a very aisle
Composed of every sort of tree —

THE FIRST WISE MAN
Still onward —

THE FOURTH WISE MAN
      Oak and beech and birch,
Like a church, but homelier than church,
The black trunks for its walls of tile;

Its roof, old leaves; its floor, beech nuts;
The squirrels its congregation —

THE SECOND WISE MAN
          Tuts!
For still we journey —

THE FOURTH WISE MAN
        But the sun weaves
A water-web across the grass,
Binding their tops. You must not pass
The water cobweb.

THE THIRD WISE MAN
       Hush! I say.
Onward and upward till the day —

THE FOURTH WISE MAN
Brother, that tree has crimson leaves.
You'll never see its like again.
Don't miss it. Look, it's bright with rain —

THE FIRST WISE MAN
O prating tongue. On, on.

THE FOURTH WISE MAN
                         And there
A toad-stool, nay, a goblin stool.
No toad sat on a thing so fair.
Wait, while I pluck — and there's — and here's
A whole ring ... what? ... berries?

(The Fourth Wise Man drops behind, botanizing.)

THE WISEST OF THE REMAINING THREE
WISE MEN
                                O fool!
Fool, fallen in this vale of tears.
His hand had touched the plough: his eyes
Looked back: no more with us, his peers,
He'll climb the hill and front the skies
And see the Star, the King, the Prize.
But we, the seekers, we who see
Beyond the mists of transiency —
Our feet down in the valley still
Are set, our eyes are on the hill.
Last night the star of God has shone,
And so we journey, up and on,
With courage clad, with swiftness shod,
All thoughts of earth behind us cast,
Until we see the lights of God,
— And what will be the crown at last?

ALL THREE WISE MEN
On, on.

(They pass on: it is already evening when the Other Wise Man limps along the road, still botanizing.)

THE OTHER WISE MAN
A vale of tears, they said!
A valley made of woes and fears,
To be passed by with muffled head
Quickly. I have not seen the tears,
Unless they take the rain for tears,
And certainly the place is wet.
Rain-laden leaves are ever licking
Your cheeks and hands ... I can't get on.
There's a toad-stool that wants picking.
There, just there, a little up,
What strange things to look upon
With pink hood and orange cup!
And there are acorns, yellow-green ...
They said the King was at the end.
They must have been
Wrong. For here, here, I intend
To search for him, for surely here
Are all the wares of the old year,
And all the beauty and bright prize,
And all God's colours meetly showed,
Green for the grass, blue for the skies,
Red for the rain upon the road;
And anything you like for trees,
But chiefly yellow, brown and gold,
Because the year is growing old
And loves to paint her children these.
I tried to follow ... but, what do you think?
The mushrooms here are pink!
And there's old clover with black polls,
Black-headed clover, black as coals,
And toad-stools, sleek as ink!
And there are such heaps of little turns
Off the road, wet with old rain:
Each little vegetable lane
Of moss and old decaying ferns,
Beautiful in decay,
Snatching a beauty from whatever may
Be their lot, dark-red and luscious: till there pass'd

Over the many-coloured earth a grey
Film. It was evening coming down at last.
And all things hid their faces, covering up
Their peak or hood or bonnet or bright cup
In greyness, and the beauty faded fast,
With all the many-coloured coat of day.
Then I looked up, and lo! the sunset sky
Had taken the beauty from the autumn earth.
Such colour, O such colour, could not die.
The trees stood black against such revelry
Of lemon-gold and purple and crimson dye.
And even as the trees, so I
Stood still and worshipped, though by evening's birth
I should have capped the hills and seen the King.
The King? The King?
I must be miles away from my journey's end;
The others must be now nearing
The summit, glad. By now they wend
Their way far, far, ahead, no doubt.
I wonder if they've reached the end.
If they have, I have not heard them shout.

1 December 1913

IX
MARLBOROUGH

I

I crouched where the open upland billows down
    Into the valley where the river flows,
She is as any other country town,
    That little lives or marks or hears or knows.

And she can teach but little. She has not
    The wonder and the surging and the roar
Of striving cities. Only things forgot
    That once were beautiful, but now no more,

Has she to give us. Yet to one or two
    She first brought knowledge, and it was for her
To open first our eyes, until we knew
    How great, immeasurably great, we were.

I, who have walked along her downs in dreams,
    And known her tenderness, and felt her might,
And sometimes by her meadows and her streams
    Have drunk deep-storied secrets of delight,

Have had my moments there, when I have been
    Unwittingly aware of something more,
Some beautiful aspect, that I had seen
    With mute unspeculative eyes before;

Have had my times, when, though the earth did wear
    Her self-same trees and grasses, I could see
The revelation that is always there,
    But somehow is not always clear to me.

II

So, long ago, one halted on his way
    And sent his company and cattle on;
His caravans trooped darkling far away
    Into the night, and he was left alone.

And he was left alone. And, lo, a man
    There wrestled with him till the break of day.
The brook was silent and the night was wan.
    And when the dawn was come, he passed away.

The sinew of the hollow of his thigh
    Was shrunken, as he wrestled there alone.
The brook was silent, but the dawn was nigh.
    The stranger named him Israel and was gone.

And the sun rose on Jacob; and he knew
    That he was no more Jacob, but had grown
A more immortal vaster spirit, who
    Had seen God face to face, and still lived on.

The plain that seemed to stretch away to God,
    The brook that saw and heard and knew no fear,
Were now the self-same soul as he who stood
    And waited for his brother to draw near.

For God had wrestled with him, and was gone.
    He looked around, and only God remained.
The dawn, the desert, he and God were one.
    — And Esau came to meet him, travel-stained.

III

So, there, when sunset made the downs look new
    And earth gave up her colours to the sky,
And far away the little city grew
    Half into sight, new-visioned was my eye.

I, who have lived, and trod her lovely earth,
    Raced with her winds and listened to her birds,
Have cared but little for their worldly worth
    Nor sought to put my passion into words.

But now it's different; and I have no rest
    Because my hand must search, dissect and spell
The beauty that is better not expressed,
    The thing that all can feel, but none can tell.

1 March 1914

X
LE REVENANT

He trod the oft-remembered lane
    (Now smaller-seeming than before
    When first he left his father's door
For newer things), but still quite plain

(Though half-benighted now) upstood
    Old landmarks, ghosts across the lane
    That brought the Bygone back again:
Shorn haystacks and the rooky wood;

The guide post, too, which once he clomb
    To read the figures: fourteen miles
    To Swindon, four to Clinton Stiles,[21]
And only half a mile to home:

And far away the one homestead, where —
    Behind the day now not quite set
    So that he saw in silhouette
Its chimneys still stand black and bare —

He noticed that the trees were not
    So big as when he journeyed last
    That way. For greatly now he passed
Striding above the hedges, hot

With hopings, as he passed by where
    A lamp before him glanced and stayed
    Across his path, so that his shade
Seemed like a giant's moving there.

---

[21] *Clinton Stiles* has not been identified and is probably imaginary. — WRS

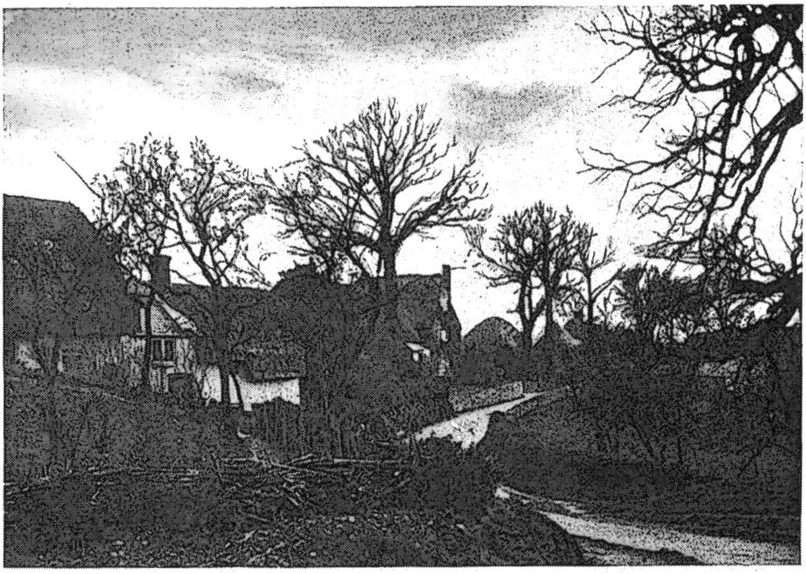

The dullness of the sunken sun
    He marked not, nor how dark it grew,
    Nor that strange flapping bird that flew
Above: he thought but of the One. . . .

He topped the crest and crossed the fence,
    Noticed the garden that it grew
    As erst, noticed the hen-house too
(The kennel had been altered since).

It seemed so unchanged and so still.
    (Could it but be the past arisen
    For one short night from out of prison?)
He reached the big-bowed window-sill,

Lifted the window sash with care,
    Then, gaily throwing aside the blind,
    Shouted. It was a shock to find
That he was not remembered there.

At once he felt not all his pain,
    But murmuringly apologised,
    Turned, once more sought the undersized
Blown trees, and the long lanky lane,

Wondering and pondering on, past where
    A lamp before him glanced and stayed
    Across his path, so that his shade
Seemed like a giant's moving there.

XI
LOST[22]

Across my past imaginings
    Has dropped a blindness silent and slow.
My eye is bent on other things
    Than those it once did see and know.

I may not think on those dear lands
    (O far away and long ago!)
Where the old battered signpost[23] stands
    And silently the four roads go

East, west, south and north,
    And the cold winter winds do blow.
And what the evening will bring forth
    Is not for me nor you to know.

December 1914

---

[22] This poem was sent to a friend in December 1914. The author wrote, "I have tried for long to express in words the impression that the land north of Marlborough must leave... Simplicity, paucity of words, monotony almost, and mystery are necessary. I think I have got it at last." Sending it home, along with a number of others, in April 1915, he described it as "the last of my Marlborough poems." —WRS

[23] the *signpost,* which figures here as well as elsewhere in the poems, stands at "the junction of the grass tracks on the Aldbourne [Poulton] downs — to Ogbourne, Marlborough, Mildenhall, and Aldbourne. It stands up quite alone." —WRS

OF SCHOOL

XII
RAIN[24]

When the rain is coming down,
And all Court[25] is still and bare,
And the leaves fall wrinkled, brown,
Through the kindly winter air,
And in tattered flannels I
'Sweat'[26] beneath a tearful sky,
And the sky is dim and grey,
And the rain is coming down,
And I wander far away
From the little red-capped town:
There is something in the rain
That would bid me to remain:
There is something in the wind
That would whisper, "Leave behind
All this land of time and rules,
Land of bells and early schools.
Latin, Greek and College food
Do you precious little good.
Leave them: if you would be free
Follow, follow, after me![27]"

---

[24] Published in *The Marlburian,* 31 October 1912.
[25] *Court,* the quadrangle, surrounded by classrooms, hall, chapel, and college houses, and intersected by a lime-tree avenue between the gate and C House. This house (to which the author belonged) was the old mansion of the Seymours, built in the middle of the seventeenth century, and is the only ancient part of the college buildings. —WRS
[26] *Sweat.* (school slang), run. —WRS
[27] *Follow, follow, after me.* From Robert Herrick's "The Fairie Queen" (1635) —BR

When I reach 'Four Miler's'[28] height,
And I look abroad again
On the skies of dirty white
And the drifting veil of rain,
And the bunch of scattered hedge
Dimly swaying on the edge,
And the endless stretch of downs
Clad in green and silver gowns;
There is something in their dress
Of bleak barren ugliness,
That would whisper, "You have read
Of a land of light and glory[29]:

But believe not what is said.
'T is a kingdom bleak and hoary,
Where the winds and tempests call
And the rain sweeps over all.
Heed not what the preachers say
Of a good land far away.
Here's a better land and kind
And it is not far to find."

---

[28] *Four Miler,* see note on poem VII.
[29] *land of light and glory*. This sermon chestnut dates back to 1855, from "The Peculiar Sleep of the Beloved," by Rev. Charles Haddon Spurgeon, who preached in musical halls to audiences of 10,000, and quoted both classics and poetry in his sermons. Herewith a sample of Spurgeon's purple prose:
"Do you know that heaven is just across that narrow stream? Are you afraid to plunge in and swim across? Do you fear to be drowned? I feel the bottom—it is good. Dost thou think thou shalt sink? Hear the voice of the Spirit: 'Fear not, I am with thee; be not dismayed, I am thy God: when thou passest through the river, I will be with thee, and the floods shall not overflow thee.' Death is the gate of endless joys, and dost thou dread to enter there? What! fear to be emancipated from corruption? Oh! say not so! but rather, gladly lay down and sleep in Jesus, and be blessed." —BR

Therefore, when we rise and sing
Of a distant land, so fine,
Where the bells for ever ring,
And the suns for ever shine:
Singing loud and singing grand,
Of a happy far-off land,
O! I smile to hear the song,
For I know that they are wrong,
That the happy land and gay
Is not very far away,
And that I can get there soon
Any rainy afternoon.

And when summer comes again,
And the downs are dimpling green,
And the air is free from rain,
And the clouds no longer seen:
Then I know that they have gone
To find a new camp further on,
Where there is no shining sun
To throw light on what is done,
Where the summer can't intrude
On the fort where winter stood:
    — Only blown and drenching grasses,
    Only rain that never passes,
    Moving mists and sweeping wind,
    And I follow them behind!

October 1912

XIII
A TALE OF TWO CAREERS[30]

I — SUCCESS

He does not dress as other men,
    His 'kish'[31] is loud and gay,
His 'side' is as the 'side' of ten
    Because his 'barnes'[32] are grey.

His head has swollen to a size
    Beyond the proper size for heads,
He metaphorically buys
    The ground on which he treads.

Before his face of haughty grace
    The ordinary mortal cowers:
A 'forty-cap'[33] has put the chap
    Into another world from ours.

---

[30] *Published in The Marlburian,* 11 November 1912. —WRS
[31] *kish* (pronounced *kish),* a flat cushion which folds double and is used by the boys as a book-carrier. The "bloods" (or athletic aristocrats of the school) affect garish colours *(loud and gay)* for the lining of their kishes. —WRS
[32] *barnes* (school slang), trousers. The school rules for dress are slightly relaxed for "bloods." —WRS
[33] *forty-cap,* for football, equivalent to about second fifteen — obtained by the author a year after these verses were written. —WRS

The funny little world that lies
    ' Twixt High Street and the Mound
Is just a swarm of buzzing flies
    That aimlessly go round:

If one is stronger in the limb
    Or better able to work hard,
It's quite amusing to watch him
    Ascending heavenward.

But if one cannot work or play
    (Who loves the better part too well),
It's really sad to see the lad
    Retained compulsorily in hell.

II — FAILURE

We are the wasters, who have no
    Hope in this world here, neither fame,
Because we cannot collar low
    Nor write a strange dead tongue the same
As strange dead men did long ago.

We are the weary, who begin
    The race with joy, but early fail,
Because we do not care to win
    A race that goes not to the frail
And humble: only the proud come in.

We are the shadow-forms, who pass
    Unheeded hence from work and play.
We are to-day, but like the grass
    That to-day is, we pass away;
And no one stops to say 'Alas!'

Though we have little, all we have
    We give our School. And no return
We can expect for what we gave;
    No joys; only a summons stern,
"Depart, for others entrance crave!"

As soon as she can clearly prove
    That from us is no hope of gain,
Because we only bring her love
    And cannot bring her strength or brain,
She tells us, "Go: it is enough."

She turns us out at seventeen,
    We may not know her any more,
And all our life with her has been
    A life of seeing others score,
While we sink lower and are mean.

We have seen others reap success
    Full-measure. None has come to us.
Our life has been one failure. Yes,
    But does not God prefer it thus?
God does not also praise success.

And for each failure that we meet,
    And for each place we drop behind,
Each toil that holds our aching feet,
    Each star we seek and never find,
God, knowing, gives us comfort meet.

The School we care for has not cared
    To cherish nor keep our names to be
Memorials. God hath prepared
    Some better thing for us, for we
His hopes have known, His failures shared.

November 1912

XIV
WHAT YOU WILL[34]

Come and see, it's such a sight,
So many boys all doing right:
To see them underneath the yoke,
Blindfolded by the elder folk,
Move at a most impressive rate
Along the way that is called straight.
O, it is comforting to know
They're in the way they ought to go.
But don't you think it's far more gay
To see them slowly leave the way

And limp and loose themselves and fall?
O, that's the nicest thing of all.
I love to see this sight, for then
I know they are becoming men,
And they are tiring of the shrine
Where things are really not divine.

I do not know if it seems brave
The youthful spirit to enslave,
And hedge about, lest it should grow.
I don't know if it's better so
In the long end. I only know
That when I have a son of mine,
He shan't be made to droop and pine,
Bound down and forced by rule and rod
To serve a God who is no God.
But I'll put custom on the shelf
And make him find his God himself.
Perhaps he'll find him in a tree,

---
[34] Published in *The Marlburian,* 10 July 1913. —WRS

Some hollow trunk, where you can see.
Perhaps the daisies in the sod
Will open out and show him God.
Or will he meet him in the roar
Of breakers as they beat the shore?
Or in the spiky stars that shine?
Or in the rain (where I found mine)?
Or in the city's giant moan?
A God who will be all his own,
To whom he can address a prayer
And love him, for he is so fair,
And see with eyes that are not dim
And build a temple meet for him.

30 June 1913

OF LIFE AND THOUGHT

XV
A CALL TO ACTION[35]

I

A thousand years have passed away,
    Cast back your glances on the scene,
Compare this England of to-day
    With England as she once has been.

Fast beat the pulse of living then:
    The hum of movement, throb of war
The rushing mighty sound of men
    Reverberated loud and far.

They girt their loins up and they trod
    The path of danger, rough and high;
For Action, Action was their god,
    "Be up and doing" was their cry.

A thousand years have passed away;
    The sands of life are running low;
The world is sleeping out her day;
    The day is dying — be it so.

A thousand years have passed amain;
The sands of life are running thin;
Thought is our leader — Thought is vain;
Speech is our goddess — Speech is sin.

---

[35] Published in *The Marlburian*, 31 October 1912. — WRS

II

It needs no thought to understand,
    No speech to tell, nor sight to see
That there has come upon our land
    The curse of Inactivity.

We do not see the vital point
    That 'tis the eighth, most deadly, sin
To wail, "The world is out of joint" —
    And not attempt to put it in.

We see the swollen stream of crime
    Flow hourly past us, thick and wide;
We gaze with interest for a time,
    And pass by on the other side.

We see the tide of human sin
    Rush roaring past our very door,
And scarcely one man plunges in
    To drag the drowning to the shore.

We, dull and dreamy, stand and blink,
    Forgetting glory, strength and pride,
Half — listless watchers on the brink,
Half — ruined victims of the tide.

III

We question, answer, make defence,
    We sneer, we scoff, we criticize,
We wail and moan our decadence,
    Enquire, investigate, surmise;

We preach and prattle, peer and pry
    And fit together two and two:
We ponder, argue, shout, swear, lie —
    We will not, for we cannot, DO.

Pale puny soldiers of the pen,
    Absorbed in this your inky strife,
Act as of old, when men were men,
    England herself and life yet life.

October 1912

XVI
PEACE[36]

There is silence in the evening when the long days cease,
And a million men are praying for an ultimate release
From strife and sweat and sorrow — they are praying
    for peace.
    But God is marching on.[37]

Peace for a people that is striving to be free!
Peace for the children of the wild wet sea!
Peace for the seekers of the promised land — do we
    Want peace when God has none?

We pray for rest and beauty that we know we cannot earn,
And ever are we asking for a honey-sweet return;
But God will make it bitter, make it bitter, till we learn
    That with tears the race is run.

And did not Jesus perish to bring to men, not peace,
But a sword, a sword for battle and a sword that should
    not cease?
Two thousand years have passed us. Do we still want peace
    Where the sword of Christ has shone?

Yes, Christ perished to present us with a sword,
That strife should be our portion and more strife
    our reward,
For toil and tribulation and the glory of the Lord
    And the sword of Christ are one.

---

[36] Published in *The Marlburian,* 19 December 1912. —WRS
[37] *God is marching on...* American readers will recognize this poem instantly as a parodic imitation of Julia Ward Howe's 1861 "Battle Hymn of the Republic." —BR

If you want to know the beauty of the thing called rest,
Go, get it from the poets, who will tell you it is best
(And their words are sweet as honey) to lie flat
     upon your chest
  And sleep till life is gone.

I know that there is beauty where the low streams run,
And the weeping of the willows and the big sunk sun,[38]
But I know my work is doing and it never shall be done,
    Though I march for ages on.

Wild is the tumult of the long grey street,
O, is it never silent from the tramping of their feet?
Here, Jesus, is Thy triumph, and here the world's defeat,
    For from here all peace has gone.

There's a stranger thing than beauty in the ceaseless
    city's breast,
In the throbbing of its fever — and the wind is
    in the west,
And the rain is driving forward where there is no rest,
    For the Lord is marching on.

December 1912

---

[38] These two lines are perhaps the only lines in the book which recall the scenery of the author's Cambridge home. —WRS

XVII
THE RIVER[39]

He watched the river running black
    Beneath the blacker sky;
It did not pause upon its track
    Of silent instancy;
It did not hasten, nor was slack,
    But still went gliding by.

It was so black. There was no wind
    Its patience to defy.
It was not that the man had sinned,
    Or that he wished to die.
Only the wide and silent tide
    Went slowly sweeping by.

The mass of blackness moving down
    Filled full of dreams the eye;
The lights of all the lighted town
    Upon its breast did lie;
The tall black trees were upside down
    In the river[40] phantasy.

---

[39] *The Marlburian,* 25 February 1913. This poem, as there printed, was preceded by the explanation, "Early in January a man, without any conceivable reason for doing so, drowned himself in the ——. The verdict at the inquest was, as is usual in such cases, 'Suicide during temporary insanity.' This is the truth." —WRS

[40] *river,* by mistake printed *river's* in editions 1 to 3. —WRS

He had an envy for its black
    Inscrutability;
He felt impatiently the lack
    Of that great law whereby
The river never travels back
    But still goes gliding by;

But still goes gliding by, nor clings
    To passing things that die,
Nor shows the secrets that it brings
    From its strange source on high.
And he felt "We are two living things
    And the weaker one is I."

He saw the town, that living stack
    Piled up against the sky.
He saw the river running black
    On, on and on: O, why
Could he not move along his track
    With such consistency?

He had a yearning for the strength
    That comes of unity:
The union of one soul at length
    With its twin-soul to lie:
To be a part of one great strength
    That moves and cannot die.

        * * *

He watched the river running black
    Beneath the blacker sky.
He pulled his coat about his back,
    He did not strive nor cry.
He put his foot upon the track
    That still went gliding by.

The thing that never travels back
    Received him silently.
And there was left no shred, no wrack
    To show the reason why:
Only the river running black
    Beneath the blacker sky.

February 1913

XVIII
THE SEEKERS[41]

The gates are open on the road
That leads to beauty and to God.

Perhaps the gates are not so fair,
Nor quite so bright as once they were,
When God Himself on earth did stand
And gave to Abraham His hand
And led him to a better land.

For lo! the unclean walk therein,
And those that have been soiled with sin.
The publican and harlot pass
Along: they do not stain its grass.
In it the needy has his share,
In it the foolish do not err.
Yes, spurned and fool and sinner stray
Along the highway and the way.[42]

And what if all its ways are trod
By those whom sin brings near to God?
This journey soon will make them clean:
Their faith is greater than their sin.

---

[41] Published in *The Marlburian,* 13 March 1913. —WRS
[42] *the highway and the way*. From *Isaiah* xxxv, 8: "And an highway shall be there, and a way, and it shall be called The way of holiness; the unclean shall not pass over it; but it shall be for those: the wayfaring men, though fools, shall not err therein." KJV —BR

For still they travel slowly by
Beneath the promise of the sky,
Scorned and rejected utterly;
Unhonoured; things of little worth
Upon the highroads of this earth;
Afflicted, destitute and weak:
Nor find the beauty that they seek,
The God they set their trust upon:
— Yet still they march rejoicing on.

March 1913

XIX
ROOKS[43]

There, where the rusty iron lies,
    The rooks are cawing all the day.
Perhaps no man, until he dies,
    Will understand them, what they say.

The evening makes the sky like clay.
    The slow wind waits for night to rise.
The world is half-content. But they

Still trouble all the trees with cries,
    That know, and cannot put away,
The yearning to the soul that flies
    From day to night, from night to day.

21 June 1913

---

[43] Published in *The Marlburian,* 10 July 1913. The rookery referred to is evidently that in the Wilderness, lying between C House and the bathing-place, and visible from the author's dormitory window. Underneath the trees in the Wilderness a good deal of rubbish *(rusty iron,* etc.) had been thrown. —WRS

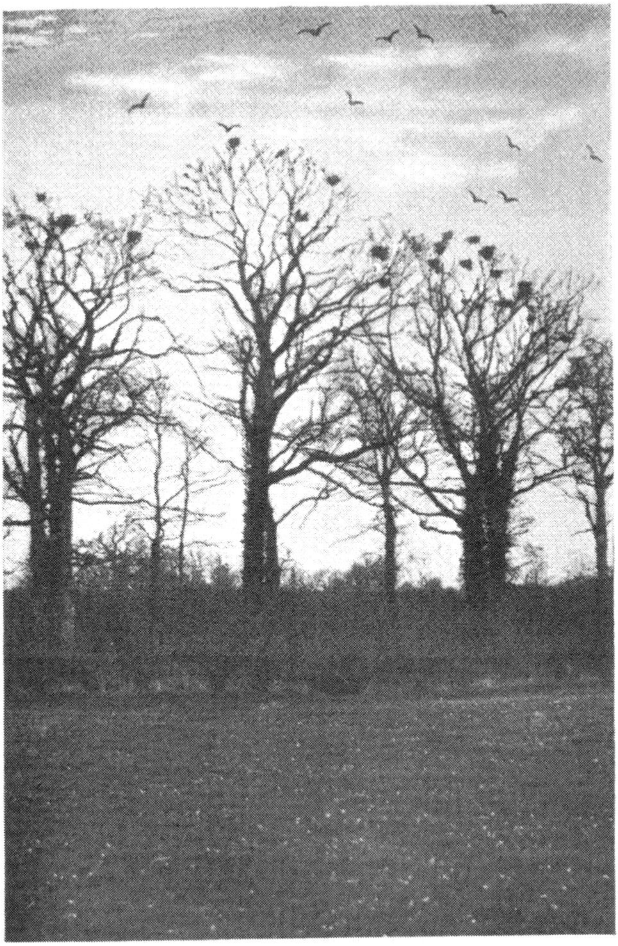

XX
ROOKS (II)[44]

There is such cry in all these birds,
    More than can ever be express'd;
If I should put it into words,
    You would agree it were not best
    To wake such wonder from its rest.

But since to-night the world is still
    And only they and I astir,
We are united, will to will,
    By bondage tighter, tenderer
    Than any lovers ever were.

And if, of too much labouring,
    All that I see around should die
(There is such sleep in each green thing,
    Such weariness in all the sky),
    We would live on, these birds and I.

Yet how? since everything must pass
    At evening with the sinking sun,
And Christ is gone, and Barabbas,
    Judas and Jesus, gone, clean gone,
    Then how shall I live on?

Yet surely Judas must have heard
    Amidst his torments the long cry
Of some lone Israelitish bird,
    And on it, ere he came to die,
    Thrown all his spirit's agony.

---

[44] Published in *The Marlburian*, 28 July 1913. —WRS

And that immortal cry which welled
    For Judas, ever afterwards
Passion on passion still has swelled
    And sweetened: so to-night these birds
    Will take my words, will take my words,

And wrapping them in music meet
    Will sing their spirit through the sky,
Strange and unsatisfied and sweet:
    That, when stock-dead am I, am I,
    O, that can never die!

25 July 1913

XXI
THE SONG OF THE UNGIRT RUNNERS

We swing ungirded[45] hips,
And lightened are our eyes,
The rain is on our lips,
We do not run for prize.
We know not whom we trust
Nor whitherward we fare,
But we run because we must
    Through the great wide air.

The waters of the seas
Are troubled as by storm.
The tempest strips the trees
And does not leave them warm.
Does the tearing tempest pause?
Do the tree-tops ask it why?
So we run without a cause
    'Neath the big bare sky.

The rain is on our lips,
We do not run for prize.
But the storm the water whips
And the wave howls to the skies.
The winds arise and strike it
And scatter it like sand,
And we run because we like it
Through the broad bright land.

---

[45] *Ungirt, ungirded.* With one's belt unfastened, undone, or absent. Perhaps this abandonment of British restraint is as close to nude athletics as Sorley and his contemporaries could get. This rapturous lyric inspired Graves's poem "Sorley's Weather." —BR

XXII
GERMAN RAIN

The heat came down and sapped away my powers.
The laden heat came down and drowsed my brain,
Till through the weight of overcoming hours
      I felt the rain.

Then suddenly I saw what more to see
I never thought: old things renewed, retrieved.
The rain that fell in England fell on me,
      And I believed.

XXIII
BRAND[46]

Thou trod'st the shifting sand path where man's race is.
The print of thy soft sandals is still clear.
I too have trodden it those prints a-near,
But the sea washes out my tired foot-traces.
And all that thou hast healed and holpen[47] here
I yearned to heal and help and wipe the tear
Away. But still I trod unpeopled spaces.
I had no twelve to follow my pure paces.
For I had thy misgivings and thy fear,
Thy crown of scorn, thy suffering's sharp spear,
Thy hopes, thy longings — only not thy dear
Love (for my crying love would no man hear),
Thy will to love, but not thy love's sweet graces,
That deep firm foothold which no sea erases.

I think that thou wast I in bygone places
In an intense eliminated year.
Now born again in days that are more drear
I wander unfulfilled: and see strange faces.

---

[46] (XXIII, XXIV), entitled in the author's manuscript "Two Songs from Ibsen's Dramatic Poems." They are not translations from Ibsen, but the author's own impressions of the dramatist's characters.—WRS

[Ibsen's "Brand" is the eponymous hero of an 1865 verse tragedy, a religious idealist who is unable to persuade others to a course of right action, doomed to be an outsider to the society he wishes to reform. —BR]

[47] *Holpen.* Past tense or past participle of "help."

XXIV
PEER GYNT[48]

When he was young and beautiful and bold
We hated him, for he was very strong.
But when he came back home again, quite old,
And wounded too, we could not hate him long.

For kingliness and conquest pranced he forth
Like some high-stepping charger bright with foam.
And south he strode and east and west and north
With need of crowns and never need of home.

Enraged we heard high tidings of his strength
And cursed his long forgetfulness. We swore
That should he come back home some eve at length,
We would deny him, we would bar the door!

And then he came. The sound of those tired feet!
And all our home and all our hearts are his,
Where bitterness, grown weary, turns to sweet,
And envy, purged by longing, pity is.

And pillows rest beneath the withering cheek,
And hands are laid the battered brows above,
And he whom we had hated, waxen weak,
First in his weakness learns a little love.

---
[48] Ibsen's 1867 drama, *Peer Gynt*, far more familiar for its stage music by Edvard Grieg than for the drama itself, covers the picaresque adventures of an ineffectual Nordic hero, merging folklore with a savage critique of the Swedish personality. —BR

XXV
TO POETS

We are the homeless, even as you,
Who hope and never can begin.
Our hearts are wounded through and through
Like yours, but our hearts bleed within.
We too make music, but our tones
'Scape not the barrier of our bones.

We have no comeliness like you.
We toil, unlovely, and we spin.
We start, return: we wind, undo:
We hope, we err, we strive, we sin,
We love: your love's not greater, but
The lips of our love's might stay shut.

We have the evil spirits too
That shake our soul with battle-din.
But we have an eviller spirit than you,
We have a dumb spirit within:
The exceeding bitter agony
But not the exceeding bitter cry.

September 1914

XXVI

If I have suffered pain
It is because I would.
I willed it. 'T is no good
To murmur or complain.
I have not served the law
That keeps the earth so fair
And gives her clothes to wear,
Raiment of joy and awe.

For all, that bow to bless
That law, shall sure abide.
But man shall not abide,
And hence his gloriousness.
Lo, evening earth doth lie
All-beauteous and all peace.
Man only does not cease
From striving[49] and from cry.

Sun sets in peace: and soon
The moon will shower her peace.
O law-abiding moon,
You hold your peace in fee![50]
Man, leastways, will not be
Down-bounden to these laws.
Man's spirit sees no cause
To serve such laws as these.

---
[49] *Man only does not cease/ From striving.* A direct reference to the one redeeming quality of the character of Faust. —BR
[50] *In fee.* As a feudal obligation. —BR

There yet are many seas
For man to wander in.
He yet must find out sin,
If aught of pleasance there
Remain for him to store,
His ravings to increase,
In quest of many a shore
Forbidden still to fare.

Peace sleeps the earth upon,
And sweet peace on the hill.
The waves that whimper still
At their long law-serving
(O flowing sad complaint!)
Come on and are back drawn.
Man only owns no king,
Man only is not faint.

You see, the earth is bound.
You see, the man is free.
For glorious liberty
He suffers and would die.
Grudge not then suffering
Or chastisemental cry.
O let his pain abound,
Earth's truant and earth's king!

XXVII
WHOM THEREFORE WE IGNORANTLY WORSHIP[51]

These things are silent. Though it may be told
Of luminous deeds that lighten land and sea,
Strong sounding actions with broad minstrelsy
Of praise, strange hazards and adventures bold,
We hold to the old things that grow not old:
Blind, patient, hungry, hopeless (without fee
Of all our hunger and unhope are we),
To the first ultimate instinct, to God we hold.

They flicker, glitter, flicker. But we bide,
We, the blind weavers of an intense fate,
Asking but this — that we may be denied:
Desiring only desire insatiate,
Unheard, unnamed, unnoticed, crucified
To our unutterable faith, we wait.

September 1914

---

[51] This poem had its origin in the author's journey from the Officers' Training Camp at Churn in Berkshire to join his regiment at Shorncliffe on 18 September 1914, when he arrived at Paddington Station shortly before the special train left which took the Marlborough boys back to school for the term. The first draft of the poem was sent to a friend soon afterwards with the words, "Enclosed the poem which eventually came out of the first day of term at Paddington. Not much trace of the origin left; but I think it should get a prize for being the first poem written since August 4th that isn't patriotic." —WRS
The draft differs in one place from the final form of the poem, and, instead of the present title, it is preceded by the verse, "And these all, having obtained a good report through faith, received not the promise."—WRS
[The title of this poem alludes to *Acts* 17:23, a passage about the "Unknown God" worshipped in Athens, and the Apostle Paul's claim that Christians were not worshipping a forbidden "foreign god," but in fact one whose temple was long established in Athens. This apostolic subterfuge adds an air of ambiguity about Sorley's intent, especially considering the circumstances of composition, on trains carrying soldiers to and from war. — BR]

XXVIII
DEUS LOQUITUR[52]

That's what I am: a thing of no desire,
With no path to discover and no plea
To offer up, so be my altar fire
May burn before the hearth continuously,
To be
For wayward men a steadfast light to see.

They know me in the morning of their days,
But ere noontide forsake me, to discern
New lore and hear new riddles. But moonrays
Bring them back footsore, humble, bent, a-burn
To turn
And warm them by my fire which they did spurn.

They flock together like tired birds. "We sought
Full many stars in many skies to see,
But ever knowledge disappointment brought.
Thy light alone, Lord, burneth steadfastly."
Ah me!
Then it is I who fain[53] would wayward be.

---

[52] *Deus loquitur*. God speaks. —BR
[53] The satiric import of Sorley's poem hinges on the meaning of "fain," which I read here to mean "rather." According to the OED, which lists "to show preference for" as a rare meaning, the word "fain" is also schoolboy slang, "in vogue among schoolboys to express a wish temporarily to withdraw from participation in the particular sport or game being played." Thus, the God of this poem would prefer to be somewhere else ("wayward") when his abject worshippers return to the ancestral altar fire. — BR

XXIX
EXPECTANS EXPECTAVI[54]

From morn to midnight, all day through,
I laugh and play as others do,
I sin and chatter, just the same
As others with a different name.

And all year long upon the stage
I dance and tumble and do rage
So vehemently, I scarcely see
The inner and eternal me.

I have a temple I do not
Visit, a heart I have forgot,
A self that I have never met,
A secret shrine — and yet, and yet

This sanctuary of my soul
Unwitting I keep white and whole,
Unlatched and lit, if Thou should'st care
To enter or to tarry there.

With parted lips and outstretched hands
And listening ears Thy servant stands,
Call Thou early, call Thou late,
To Thy great service dedicate.

May 1915

---

[54] Published posthumously in *The Times Literary Supplement,* 28 October 1915. This is the Latin title of Psalm 40, "I waited patiently for the Lord." Compare Sorley's text with the hymn to see the parallels in theme and content. Sorley's poem was set as a church anthem by Charles Wood in 1919. — BR

OF WAR AND DEATH

XXX[55]

All the hills and vales along
Earth is bursting into song,
And the singers are the chaps
Who are going to die perhaps.
    O sing, marching men,
    Till the valleys ring again.
    Give your gladness to earth's keeping,
    So be glad, when you are sleeping.

Cast away regret and rue,
Think what you are marching to.
Little live, great pass.
Jesus Christ and Barabbas
Were found the same day.
This died, that went his way.
    So sing with joyful breath,
    For why, you are going to death.
    Teeming earth will surely store
    All the gladness that you pour.

Earth that never doubts nor fears,
Earth that knows of death, not tears,
Earth that bore with joyful ease
Hemlock for Socrates,
Earth that blossomed and was glad
'Neath the cross that Christ had,
Shall rejoice and blossom too
When the bullet reaches you.
    Wherefore, men marching
    On the road to death, sing!
    Pour your gladness on earth's head,
    So be merry, so be dead.

---

[55] There is external evidence, though it is not quite conclusive, for dating this poem in August 1914. —WRS

From the hills and valleys earth
Shouts back the sound of mirth,
Tramp of feet and lilt of song
Ringing all the road along.
All the music of their going,
Ringing swinging glad song-throwing,
Earth will echo still, when foot
Lies numb and voice mute.
   On, marching men, on
   To the gates of death with song.
   Sow your gladness for earth's reaping,
   So you may be glad, though sleeping.
   Strew your gladness on earth's bed,
   So be merry, so be dead. [56]

---

[56] This poem inverts the war-fever of other poets who issued valedictory poems sending men off to battle. Compare this to Thomas Hardy's jingoistic "Men Who March Away" of 1914 or Julian Grenfell's "Into Battle," which promises the soldier the "Joy of Battle." Both Hardy's and Grenfell's poems have jingling rhymes and a near absence of enjambment, apparently intended for musical setting, and Sorley adopts a similar mode here, although he is not as adept at avoiding enjambed lines..

XXXI
TO GERMANY[57]

You are blind like us. Your hurt no man designed,
And no man claimed the conquest of your land.
But gropers both through fields of thought confined
We stumble and we do not understand.
You only saw your future bigly planned,
And we, the tapering paths of our own mind,
And in each other's dearest ways we stand,
And hiss and hate. And the blind fight the blind.

When it is peace, then we may view again
With new-won eyes each other's truer form
And wonder. Grown more loving-kind and warm
We'll grasp firm hands and laugh at the old pain,
When it is peace. But until peace, the storm
The darkness and the thunder and the rain.

---
[57] There is the same evidence for dating this poem also in August 1914.— WRS

XXXII

A hundred thousand million mites we go
Wheeling and tacking o'er the eternal plain,
Some black with death — and some are white with woe.
Who sent us forth? Who takes us home again?

And there is sound of hymns of praise — to whom?
And curses — on whom curses? — snap the air.
And there is hope goes hand in hand with gloom,
And blood and indignation and despair.

And there is murmuring of the multitude
And blindness and great blindness, until some
Step forth and challenge blind Vicissitude
Who tramples on them: so that fewer come.

And nations, ankle-deep in love or hate,
Throw darts or kisses all the unwitting hour
Beside the ominous unseen tide of fate;
And there is emptiness and drink and power.

And some are mounted on swift steeds of thought
And some drag sluggish feet of stable toil.
Yet all, as though they furiously sought,
Twist turn and tussle, close and cling and coil.

A hundred thousand million mites we sway
Writhing and tossing on the eternal plain,
Some black with death — but most are bright with Day!
Who sent us forth? Who brings us home again?

September 1914

XXXIII
TWO SONNETS[58]

I

Saints have adored the lofty soul of you.
Poets have whitened at your high renown.
We stand among the many millions who
Do hourly wait to pass your pathway down.
You, so familiar, once were strange: we tried
To live as of your presence unaware.
But now in every road on every side
We see your straight and steadfast signpost there.

I think it like that signpost in my land,
Hoary and tall, which pointed me to go
Upward, into the hills, on the right hand,
Where the mists swim and the winds shriek and blow,
A homeless land and friendless, but a land
I did not know and that I wished to know.

---

[58] A copy of the former of these two sonnets was sent to a friend with the title "Death and the Downs." The title in the book is taken from the copy sent home by the author. —WRS

II

Such, such is Death: no triumph: no defeat:
Only an empty pail, a slate rubbed clean,
A merciful putting away of what has been.

And this we know: Death is not Life effete,
Life crushed, the broken pail. We who have seen
So marvellous things know well the end not yet.

Victor and vanquished are a-one in death:
Coward and brave: friend, foe. Ghosts do not say
"Come, what was your record when you drew breath?"
But a big blot has hid each yesterday
So poor, so manifestly incomplete.
And your bright Promise, withered long and sped,
Is touched, stirs, rises, opens and grows sweet
And blossoms and is you, when you are dead.

12 June 1915

XXXIV[59]

When you see millions of the mouthless dead
Across your dreams in pale battalions go,
Say not soft things as other men have said,[60]
That you'll remember. For you need not so.
Give them not praise. For, deaf, how should they know
It is not curses heaped on each gashed head?
Nor tears. Their blind eyes see not your tears flow.
Nor honour. It is easy to be dead.
Say only this, "They are dead." Then add thereto,
"Yet many a better one has died before."
Then, scanning all the o'ercrowded mass, should you
Perceive one face that you loved heretofore,
It is a spook. None wears the face you knew.
Great death has made all his for evermore.

---

[59] This sonnet was found in the author's kit sent home from France after his death. —WRS

[60] *As other men have said...* The "soft things" said may be a Lucretian rebuttal to Rupert Brooke's famous sonnet "The Soldier," which evokes flowers and English air, and the dead adding a bit of English dust to a foreign field. Sorley's poem is the antithesis of Brooke's sentimentality.

XXXV[61]

There is such change in all those fields,
Such motion rhythmic, ordered, free,
Where ever-glancing summer yields
Birth, fragrance, sunlight, immanency,
To make us view our rights of birth.
What shall we do? How shall we die?
We, captives of a roaming earth,
'Mid shades that life and light deny.
Blank summer's surfeit heaves in mist;
Dumb earth basks dewy-washed; while still
We whom Intelligence has kissed
Do make us shackles of our will.
And yet I know in each loud brain,
Round-damped with laws and learning so,
Is madness more and lust of strain

Than earth's jerked godlings e'er can know.
The false Delilah of our brain
Has set us round the millstone going.
O lust of roving! lust of pain!
Our hair will not be long in growing.
Like blinded Samson[62] round we go.
We hear the grindstone groan and cry.
Yet we are kings, we know, we know.
What shall we do? How shall we die?
Take but our pauper's gift of birth,
O let us from the grindstone free!
And tread the maddening gladdening earth

---
[61] This poem was sent to a friend in July 1915. It appeared for the first time in the second edition. —WRS
[62] *Samson.* The story of Samson and Delilah is related in the *Book of Judges* 13-16. The Herculean hero Samson, seduced and betrayed by the Philistine temptress Delilah, is blinded and chained to a millstone. Shorn of the long hair that gave him his strength, he is able to defeat his adversaries only after his hair grows back. The Samson story is also related in Josephus' *Antiquities of the Jews* (94 CE); retold in Milton's *Samson Agonistes* (1671); set to music in Handel's *Samson* (1743, based on Milton) and staged as opera in Saint-Saens' *Samson et Delilah* (1877). —BR

In strength close-braced with purity.
The earth is old; we ever new.
Our eyes should see no other sense
Than this, eternally to DO —
Our joy, our task, our recompense;
Up unexplorèd mountains move,
Track tireless through great wastes afar,
Nor slumber in the arms of love,
Nor tremble on the brink of war;
Make Beauty and make Rest give place,
Mock Prudence loud — and she is gone,
Smite Satisfaction on the face
And tread the ghost of Ease upon.
Light-lipped and singing press we hard
Over old earth which now is worn,
Triumphant, buffeted and scarred,
By billows howled at, tempest-torn,
Toward blue horizons far away
(Which do not give the rest we need,
But some long strife, more than this play,
Some task that will be stern indeed) —
We ever new, we ever young,[63]
We happy creatures of a day![64]
What will the gods say, seeing us strung
As nobly and as taut as they?

---

[63] *We ever new, we ever young.* A line from the hymn, "Awake, our souls, away, our tears" by Isaac Watts (1709). One of the alternate tunes for the hymn is taken from Handel's *Samson,* which may have kindled the association in Sorley's memory. —BR

[64] *Creatures of a day.* From Pindar (446 BCE): "Creatures of a day! What is anyone? What is he not? Man is but a dream of a shadow; but when a gleam of sunshine cometh as a gift of heaven, a radiant light resteth on men, aye, and a gentle life." (*Pythian Odes* viii, 95-8) —BR

XXXVI[65]

I have not brought my *Odyssey*
With me here across the sea;
But you'll remember, when I say
How, when they went down Sparta way,
To sandy Sparta, long ere dawn
Horses were harnessed, rations drawn,
Equipment polished sparkling bright,
And breakfasts swallowed (as the white
Of Eastern heavens turned to gold) —
The dogs barked, swift farewells were told.
The sun springs up, the horses neigh,
Crackles the whip thrice — then away!
From sun-go-up to sun-go-down
All day across the sandy down
The gallant horses galloped, till
The wind across the downs more chill
Blew, the sun sank and all the road
Was darkened, that it only showed
Right at the end the town's red light
And twilight glimmering into night.

---

[65] The epistle in verse (fragments of which have been communicated to the editor and are printed here) was sent anonymously to J[ohn] B[ain]. (see note to VII). He discovered the authorship by sending the envelope of the letter to a Marlborough master, and replied in the beautiful verses which the editor is allowed to quote:

From far away there comes a Voice,
Singing its song across the sea —
A song to make man's heart rejoice —
Of Marlborough and the Odyssey.
A Voice that sings of Now and Then,
Of minstrel joys and tiny towns,
Of flowering thyme and fighting men,
Of Sparta's sands and Marlborough's Downs.

God grant, dear Voice, one day again
We see those Downs in April weather,
And snuff the breeze and smell the rain,
And stand in C House Porch together. — WRS

The horses never slackened till
They reached the doorway and stood still.
Then came the knock, the unlading; then
The honey-sweet converse of men,

The splendid bath, the change of dress,
Then — O the grandeur of their Mess,
The henchmen, the prim stewardess!
And O the breaking of old ground,
The tales, after the port went round!
(The wondrous wiles of old Odysseus,
Old Agamemnon and his misuse
Of his command, and that young chit
Paris — who didn't care a bit
For Helen — only to annoy her
He did it really, *K.T.L.*[66]

But soon they led amidst the din
The honey-sweet *aoidos*[67] in,
Whose eyes were blind, whose soul had sight,
Who knew the fame of men in fight —
Bard of white hair and trembling foot,
Who sang whatever God might put
Into his heart.
              And there he sung,
Those war-worn veterans among,
Tales of great war and strong hearts wrung,
Of clash of arms, of council's brawl,
Of beauty that must early fall,
Of battle hate and battle joy
By the old windy walls of Troy.
They felt that they were unreal then,
Visions and shadow-forms, not men.
But those the Bard did sing and say
(Some were their comrades, some were they)
Took shape and loomed and strengthened more
Greatly than they had guessed of yore.

---

[66] *K.T.L.* Greek, *kai ta loipa*. Translates as "Et cetera." —WRS
[67] *Aiodos*. Greek, *aoidos*, bard or minstrel. —WRS

And now the fight begins again,
The old war-joy, the old war-pain.
Sons of one school across the sea
We have no fear to fight —

* * * * * *

And soon, O soon, I do not doubt it,
With the body or without it,
We shall all come tumbling down
To our old wrinkled red-capped town.
Perhaps the road up Ilsley[68] way,
The old ridge-track, will be my way.

High up among the sheep and sky,
Look down on Wantage, passing by,
And see the smoke from Swindon town;
And then full left at Liddington,
Where the four winds of heaven meet
The earth-blest traveller to greet.
And then my face is toward the south,
There is a singing on my mouth:
Away to rightward I descry
My Barbury ensconced in sky,
Far underneath the Ogbourne twins,[69]
And at my feet the thyme and whins,
The grasses with their little crowns
Of gold, the lovely Aldbourne downs,[70]
And that old signpost (well I knew
That crazy signpost, arms askew,
Old mother of the four grass ways).

---

68 *Ilsley*, about 20 miles due east of Swindon and on the northern slope of the Berkshire downs. —WRS
69 *the Ogbourne twins*. Ogbourne St. George and Ogbourne St. Andrew, villages in the Valley of the Og, about five and three miles respectively north of Marlborough. —WRS
70 *Aldbourne downs*, on the Eastern side of the Og and adjoining the Marlborough downs. —WRS

And then my mouth is dumb with praise,
For, past the wood and chalkpit tiny,
A glimpse of Marlborough *erateini*![71]
So I descend beneath the rail
To warmth and welcome and wassail.

    * * * * * *

This from the battered trenches — rough,
Jingling and tedious enough.
And so I sign myself to you:

One, who some crooked pathways knew
Round Bedwyn[72]: who could scarcely leave
The Downs on a December eve:
Was at his happiest in shorts,
And got-not many good reports!
Small skill of rhyming in his hand —
But you'll forgive — you'll understand.

12 July 1915

---

[71] *Erateini*. Greek: lovely. —WRS
[72] *Bedwyn*. Great and Little Bedwyn, about a mile from the Southeastern corner of Savernake forest and about six miles from Marlborough. —WRS

XXXVII
IN MEMORIAM[73]

S.C.W.[74], *V.C.*[75]

There is no fitter end than this.
    No need is now to yearn nor sigh.
We know the glory that is his,
    A glory that can never die.

Surely we knew it long before,
    Knew all along that he was made
For a swift radiant morning, for
    A sacrificing swift night-shade.

8 September 1915

---

[73] Published posthumously in *The Marlburian*, 24 November 1915. —WRS

[74] *S.C.W.* Sidney Clayton Woodroffe, killed in action at Hooge on 30 July 1915 and awarded a posthumous V.C., was a school contemporary of the author. —WRS

[75] *V.C.* Victoria Cross.

XXXVIII
BEHIND THE LINES[76]

We are now at the end of a few days' rest, a kilometre behind the lines. Except for the farmyard noises (new style) it might almost be the little village that first took us to its arms six weeks ago. It has been a fine day, following on a day's rain, so that the earth smells like spring. I have just managed to break off a long conversation with the farmer in charge, a tall thin stooping man with sad eyes, in trouble about his land: *les Anglais* stole his peas, trod down his corn and robbed his young potatoes: he told it as a father telling of infanticide. There may have been fifteen francs' worth of damage done; he will never get compensation out of those shifty Belgian burgomasters; but it was not exactly the fifteen francs but the invasion of the soil that had been his for forty years, in which the weather was his only enemy, that gave him a kind of Niobe's[77] dignity to his complaint.

Meanwhile there is the usual evening sluggishness. Close by, a quickfirer[78] is pounding away its allowance of a dozen shells a day. It is like a cow coughing. Eastward there begins a sound (all sounds begin at sundown and continue intermittently till midnight, reaching their zenith at about 9 p.m. and then dying away as sleepiness claims their masters) — a sound like a motor-cycle race — thousands of motor-cycles tearing round and round a track, with cut-outs out: it is really a pair of machine guns firing. And now one sound awakens another. The old cow coughing has started the motor-bykes: and now at intervals of a few minutes come express trains in our direction: you can hear them rushing toward us; they pass

---
[76] This prose description is extracted from a letter home. The title has been supplied by the editor.—WRS [The letter is dated 15 July 1915; the Battle of Loos in which Sorley was killed commenced on 25 September. —BR]

[77] *Niobe*. In Ovid's *Metamorphoses*, a perennially weeping queen, whose fourteen children were slain by Apollo and Artemis. —BR

[78] *Quickfirer*. Rapid-firing, short-barrel howitzer gun, typically used for firing short distances against massed troops. Sorley's "dozen shells a day" conveys its virtual uselessness without an endless supply of ammunition. —BR

going straight for the town behind us: and you hear them begin to slow down as they reach the town: they will soon stop: but no, every time, just before they reach it, is a tremendous railway accident. At least, it must be a railway accident, there is so much noise, and you can see the dust that the wreckage scatters. Sometimes the train behind comes very close, but it too smashes on the wreckage of its forerunners. A tremendous cloud of dust, and then the groans. So many trains and accidents start the cow coughing again: only another cow this time, somewhere behind us, a tremendous-sized cow, *thaumasion oson,*[79] with awful whooping-cough. It must be a buffalo: this cough must burst its sides. And now someone starts sliding down the stairs on a tin tray, to soften the heart of the cow, make it laugh and cure its cough. The din he makes is appalling. He is beating the tray with a broom now, every two minutes a stroke: he has certainly stopped the cow by this time, probably killed it. He will leave off soon (thanks to the "shell tragedy"[80]): we know he can't last.

It is now almost dark: come out and see the fireworks. While waiting for them to begin you can notice how pale and white the corn[81] is in the summer twilight: no wonder with all this whooping-cough about. And the motor-cycles: notice how all these races have at least a hundred entries: there is never a single cycle going. And why are there no birds coming back to roost? Where is the lark? I haven't heard him all to-day. He must have got whooping-cough as well, or be staying at home through fear of the cow. I think it will rain tomorrow, but there have been no swallows circling low, stroking their breasts on the full ears of corn. Anyhow, it is night now, but the circus does not close till twelve. Look! there is the first of them! The

---

[79] *thaumasion oson*. Wonderfully great. A common expression found in Plutarch and other Greek writers. It seems to have acquired satiric status among scholars as early as the 17th century, when Urquhart describes how the infant giant Pantagruel causes his mother's death during childbirth: "so wonderfully great and lumpish that he could not possibly come forth into the light of the world without thus suffocating his mother."—BR

[80] *Shell tragedy*. A severe shortage of artillery shells, documented as a major cause of the failure of the ensuing battle.—BR

[81] *Corn*. Not American maize corn, but grain such as wheat, rye or barley. —BR

fireworks are beginning. Red flares shooting up high into the night, or skimming low over the ground, like the swallows that are not: and rockets bursting into stars. See how they illumine that patch of ground a mile in front. See it, it is deadly pale in their searching light: ghastly, I think, and featureless except for two big lines of eyebrows ashy white, parallel along it, raised a little from its surface. Eyebrows. Where are the eyes? Hush, there are no eyes. What those shooting flares illumine is a mole. A long thin mole. Burrowing by day, and shoving a timorous enquiring snout above the ground by night. Look, did you see it? No, you cannot see it from here. But were you a good deal nearer, you would see behind that snout a long and endless row of sharp shining teeth. The rockets catch the light from these teeth and the teeth glitter: they are silently removed from the poison-spitting gums of the mole. For the mole's gums spit fire and, they say, send something more concrete than fire darting into the night. Even when its teeth are off. But you cannot see all this from here: you can only see the rockets and then for a moment the pale ground beneath. But it is quite dark now.

And now for the fun of the fair! You will hear soon the riding-master crack his whip — why, there it is. Listen, a thousand whips are cracking, whipping the horses round the ring. At last! The fun of the circus is begun. For the motor-cycle team race has started off again: and the whips are cracking all: and the waresman starts again, beating his loud tin tray to attract the customers: and the cows in the cattle-show start coughing, coughing: and the firework display is at its best: and the circus specials come one after another bearing the merry-makers back to town, all to the inevitable crash, the inevitable accident. It can't last long: these accidents are so frequent, they'll all get soon killed off, I hope. Yes, it is diminishing. The train service is cancelled (and time too): the cows have stopped coughing: and the cycle race is done. Only the kids who have bought new whips at the fair continue to crack them: and unused rockets that lie about the ground are still sent up occasionally. But now the children are being driven off to bed: only an occasional whip-crack now (perhaps the child is now the sufferer): and the tired showmen going over the ground pick up the rocket-sticks and dead flares. At least I suppose this is what must be happening: for occasionally they still find one that has not gone off and send it up out of mere perversity. Else what silence!

It must be midnight now. Yes, it is midnight. But before you go to bed, bend down, put your ear against the ground. What do you hear? "I hear an endless tapping and a tramping to and fro: both are muffled: but they come from everywhere. Tap, tap, tap: pick, pick, pick: tra-mp, tra-mp, tra-mp." So you see the circus-goers are not all gone to sleep. There is noise coming from the womb of earth, noise of men who tap and mine[82] and dig and pass to and fro on their watch. What you have seen is the foam and froth of war: but underground is labour and throbbing and long watch. Which will one day bear their fruit. They will set the circus on fire. Then what pandemonium! Let us hope it will not be tomorrow!

15 July 1915

---

[82] *Men who tap and mine.* Sorley refers here to the Corp of Royal Engineers, the "Sappers," whose tunneling activities were a key part of the preparation for the coming battle. —BR

ILLUSTRATIONS IN PROSE

I
RICHARD JEFFERIES (p. 16)

I am sweatily struggling[83] to the end of *Faust II*[84], where Goethe's just showing off his knowledge. I am also reading a very interesting book on Goethe and Schiller; very adoring it is, but it lets out quite unconsciously the terrible dryness of their entirely intellectual friendship and (Goethe's at least) entirely intellectual life. If Goethe really died saying "more light," it was very silly of him: what *he* wanted was more warmth. G. and S. apparently made friends, on their own confession, merely because their ideas and artistic ideals were the same, which fact ought to be the very first to make them bore one another.

All this is leading to the following conclusion.

The Germans can act Shakespeare, have good beer and poetry, but their prose is cobwebby stuff. Hence I want to read some good prose again. Also it is summer. And for a year or two I had always laid up "The Pageant of Summer" as a treat for a hot July. In spite of all former vows of celibacy in the way of English, now's the time. So, unless the cost of book-postage here is ruinous, could you send me a small volume of Essays by Richard Jefferies called *The Life of the Fields,* the first essay in the series being the Pageant of Summer? No particular hurry, but I should be amazingly grateful if you'll send it (it's quite a little book), especially as I presume the pageant of summer takes place in that part of the country where I should be now had ——— had a stronger will than you. In the midst

---

[83] *sweatily struggling*. Nietzsche's *The Case of Wagner*, available in English as early as 1899, introduced the idea that one "sweats" while listening to Wagner's operas. This was quickly paraphrased to "Wagner sweats" and became a catch-all for the *gravitas* and ponderousness of high German art. —BR

[84] Part II of *Faust* was published in 1832, nearly a quarter century after Part I. Unlike Part I, with its focus on the seduction of Gretchen and the bargain between Faust and Mephistopheles, Part II is a rambling, philosophical and political work ending with the apotheosis of Faust, whose soul Goethe was not willing to turn over to the Devil despite Faust having lost his wager. *Faust II* is not easy reading in German or in translation. Now, as then, many English students learn German by reading Goethe. —BR

of my setting up and smashing of deities — Masefield, Hardy, Goethe — I always fall back on Richard Jefferies wandering about in the background. I have at least the tie of locality with him. *(July 1914)*

I've given up German prose altogether. It's like a stale cake compounded of foreign elements. So I have laid in a huge store of Richard Jefferies for the rest of July, and read him none the less voraciously because we are countrymen. (I know it's wrong of me, but I count myself as Wiltshire. . . .) When I die (in sixty years) I am going to leave all my presumably enormous fortune to Marlborough on condition that a thorough knowledge of Richard Jefferies is ensured by the teaching there. I think it is only right considering we are bred upon the self-same hill. It would also encourage Naturalists and discourage cricketers.[85] . . .

But, in any case, I'm not reading so much German as I did ought to. I dabble in their modern poetry[86], which is mostly of the morbidly religious kind. The language is massively beautiful, the thought is rich and sleek, the air that of the inside of a church. Magnificent artists they are, with no inspiration, who take religion up as a very responsive subject for art, and mould it in their hands like sticky putty. There are magnificent parts in it, but you can imagine what a relief it was to get back to Jefferies and Liddington Castle. *(July 1914)*

---

[85] *cricketers*. The intrusion of fields and spectator areas for the sport of cricket into Wiltshire would have been anathema to Jefferies. —BR

[86] Modern poetry. Sorley was reading Rilke and Hölderlin. —BR

II
IBSEN (pp. 63-64)

Ibsen's last, *John Gabriel Borkman*[87], is a wonderfully fine play, far better than any others by Ibsen that I have read or seen, but I can imagine it would lose a good deal in an English translation[88]. The acting of the two middle-aged sisters who are the protagonists was marvellous. The men were a good deal more difficult to hear, but also very striking. Next to the fineness of the play (which has far more poetry in it than any others of his I've read, though of course there's a bank in the background, as there always seems to be in Ibsen) — the apathy of the very crowded house struck me most. There was very little clapping at the end of the acts: at the end of the play none, which was just as well because one of them was dead and would have had to jump up again. So altogether I am very much struck by my first German theatre, though the fineness of the play may have much to do with it. It was just a little spoilt by the last Act being in a pine forest on a hill with sugar that was meant to look like snow. This rather took away from the effect of the scene, which in the German is one of the finest things I have ever heard, possessing throughout a wonderful rhythm which may or may not exist in the original. What a beautiful language it can be! (*13 February* 1914)

I have been reading many criticisms of *John Gabriel Borkman,* and it strikes me more and more that it is the most remarkable play I have ever read. It is head and shoulders above the others of Ibsen's I know: a much broader affair. John Gabriel Borkman is a tremendous character. His great desire, which led him to overstep the law for one moment, and of course he was caught and got eight years, was "*Menschenglück zu schaffen.*[89]" One moment Ibsen lets you see one side of his character (the side he himself saw) and you see the Perfect

---

[87] *John Gabriel Borkman*, actually Ibsen's penultimate play, was published in 1896, and had its first London performance in 1897. The play was never a success on stage, so the audience silence Sorley reports may not be solely a "German" phenomenon.—BR

[88] Sorley is seeing Ibsen's Norwegian plays in German performances, and, we assume, reading Ibsen in German.—BR

[89] *Menschenglück zu schaffen*. To bring about human happiness.—WRS

Altruist: the next moment the other side is turned, and you see the Complete Egoist. The play all takes place in the last three hours of J.G.B.'s life, and in these three hours his real love, whom he had rejected for business reasons and married her twin-sister, shows him for the first time the Egoist that masqueraded all its life as Altruist. The technique is perfect and it bristles with minor problems. It is absolutely fair, for if J.G.B. had sacrificed his ideals and married the right twin, he would not have been deserted after his disgrace. And the way that during the three hours the whole past history of the man comes out is marvellous. The brief dialogue between the sisters which closes the piece is fine, and suddenly throws a new light on the problem of how the tragedy could have been evaded, when you thought all that could be said had been said. (*20 February* 1914)

I feel that this visit to Schwerin[90] will spoil me for the theatre for the rest of my life. I have never ceased to see *John Gabriel Borkman* mentally since my second visit to it (when the acting was even finer than before and struck me as a perfect presentation of a perfect play). My only regret was that the whole family wasn't there as well. I should so like to talk it over with you, and the way that at the very end of his last play Ibsen sums up the object against which all his battle was directed: "Es war viel mehr die Kälte die ihn tötete." "Die Kälte, sagst du, die Kälte! die hat ihn schon längst getötet." . . . "Ja, die Herzenskälte[91]." (*10 April* 1914)

[The play] at the Königliches Schauspielhauss[92] [Berlin] was Ibsen's *Peer Gynt* with Grieg's incidental music — the Northern Faust, as it is called: though the mixture of allegory and reality is not carried off so successfully as in the Southern Faust.

Peer Gynt has the advantage of being a far more human and amiable creature, and not a cold fish like Faust. I suppose that difference is also to be found in the characters of the respective authors. I always wanted to know why Faust had no relations to make demands on him[93]. Peer Gynt is a

---

[90] Probably the Staatstheater (City Theater) in Schwerin. —BR
[91] It was rather the cold that killed him." "The cold, say you, the cold! Why, that killed him long ago." ... " Yes, coldness of heart." —WRS
[92] Royal Theatre. —WRS

charmingly light piece, with an irresistible mixture of fantastical poetry and a very racy humour. The scene where Peer returns to his blind and dying mother and, like a practical fellow, instead of sentimentalizing, sits himself on the end of her bed, persuades her it is a chariot and rides her up to heaven, describing the scenes on the way, the surliness of St Peter at the gate, the appearance of God the Father, who "put Peter quite in the shade" and decided to let mother Aasa in, was delightful. The acting was of course perfect. *(5 June* 1914)

---

[93] Sorley disregards the fact that Doctor Faust is a very old man at the beginning of *Faust I*, later restored to youth by a bargain with the Devil.—BR

III
THE ODYSSEY (p. 82)

The *Odyssey* is a great joy when once you can read it in big chunks and not a hundred lines at a time, being [forced] to note all the silly grammatical strangenesses. I could not read it in better surroundings for the whole tone of the book is so thoroughly German and domestic. A friend of sorts of the [Beutin]s died lately; and when the Frau attempted to break the news to Karl at table, he immediately said "Don't tell me anything sad while I'm eating." That very afternoon I came across someone in the *Odyssey* who made, under the same circumstances, precisely the same remark.[94] In the *Odyssey* and in Schwerin alike they are perfectly unaffected about their devotion to good food. In both too I find the double patriotism which suffers not a bit from its duplicity — in the *Odyssey* to their little Ithaca as well as to Achaea as a whole; here equally to the Kaiser and the pug-nosed Grand Duke. In both is the habit of longwinded anecdotage in the same rambling irrelevant way, and the quite unquenchable hospitality. And the Helen of the *Odyssey* bustling about a footstool for Telemachus or showing off her new presents (she had just returned from a jaunt to Egypt[95]) — a washing-tub, a spindle, and a work-

---

[94] *Odyssey*, IV, 193, 194. —WRS

[95] Menelaus and Helen had a delayed return to Greece after the Trojan War, including an unintended visit to Egypt, a vagary of ancient sea travel before the compass. Somehow Menelaus profited from the Egyptian side trip, in addition to whatever loot he had brought from Troy. Sorley here may also be alluding to the wry claim that Helen had never been disloyal to her husband at all and had never been at Troy. A fragment from Stesichoros (f 191), in the sixth century BCE, introduces the legend of "The Egyptian Helen" who had waited out the war in wifely purity while the Greeks and Trojans fought over a phantom (a substitution to which Paris was none the wiser,) and Euripides adapted this wry deception in his drama, *Helen,* in 412 BCE. Perhaps most pertinent to understanding Sorley, we must recall that he was reading Goethe's *Faust II* throughout 1914 and 1915: the entire third act of *Faust II* is devoted to Faust's wooing, and marrying, an idealized recreation (a twin or double), of Helen of Troy. *The Egyptian Helen* was adapted as an opera by in 1928 by Richard Strauss, demonstrating the allure of this legend.—BR

basket that ran on wheels (think!) — is the perfect German Hausfrau. (*27 March* 1914*)*

If I had the smallest amount of patience, steadiness or concentrative faculty, I could write a brilliant book comparing life in Ithaca, Sparta and holy Pylos in the time of Odysseus with life in Mecklenburg-Schwerin in the time of Herr Dr [Beutin]. In both you get the same unquenchable hospitality and perfectly unquenchable anecdotage faculty. In both whenever you make a visit or go into a house, they are "busying themselves with a meal." Du lieber Karl (I mean Herr Dr. [Beutin]) has three times, when his wife has tried to talk of death, disease or crime [at] table, unconsciously given a literal translation of Peisistratus's[96] sound remark *ou gar ego ge terpom odyromenos metadorpios*[97] — and that is their attitude to meals throughout. Need I add the *aglaa dora*[98] they insist on giving their guests, with the opinion that it is the host that is the indebted party and the possession of a guest confers honour and responsibility: and their innate patriotism, the *ou toi ego ge ēs gaiēs dynamai glykeroteron allo idesthai*[99] spirit (however dull it is) to complete the parallel? So I am really reading it in sympathetic surroundings, and when I have just got past the part where Helen shows off to Menelaus her new work-basket that runs on wheels, and the Frau rushes in to show me her new water-can with a spout designed to resemble a pig — I see the two are made from the same stuff (I mean, of course, Helen and Frau [Beutin], not Frau [Beutin] and the pig). Also, I enjoy being able to share in a quiet amateur way with Odysseus his feelings about "were it but the smoke leaping up from his own land."[100] (*23 April* 1914)

Good luck to Helen of Troy. As you say, she loved her own sex as well. Her last appearance in Homer is when

---

[96] *Peisistratus.* Young companion of Telemachus who accompanies him on his search for his father. —BR

[97] *ou gar ego ge terpom odyromenos metadorpios.* I do not like having to lament during supper. —*Odyssey,* IV, 193, 194. —WRS

[98] *aglaa dora.* Splendid gifts. —WRS

[99] *ou toi ego...* I for my part can see nothing sweeter than one's own country. —*Odyssey,* IX, 27, 28. —WRS

[100] *were it but the smoke...* From *The Odyssey*, Book I.

Telemachus was just leaving her and Menelaus after paying them a visit in Sparta, "and she stood on the doorstep with a robe in her hand and spoke a word and called him, 'I also am giving thee a gift, dear child, — this, a memorial of Helen's handiwork, against the day of thy marriage to which we all look forward, that thou mayest give it to thy wife: till then, let it be stored in thy palace under thy mother's care.'" But she never gives to me the impression in Homer of being quite happy. I'm sure she was always dull down in Sparta with fatherly old Menelaus — though she never showed it of course. But there is always something a little wistful in her way of speaking. She only made other people happy and consequently another set of other people miserable. One of the best things in the *Iliad* is the way you are made to feel (without any statement) that Helen fell really in love with Hector — and this shows her good taste, for of all the Homeric heroes Hector is the only unselfish man. She seems to me only to have loved to please Menelaus and Paris but to have really loved Hector — and naturally, for Hector and Achilles, the altruist and the egoist, were miles nobler than anyone else on either side — but Hector never gave any sign that he regarded her as anything more than his distressed sister-in-law. But after Hector's death she must have left part of her behind her, and made a real nice wife to poor pompous Menelaus in his old age. She seems to have had a marvelous power of adaptability. *(April* 1914)

I made my pilgrimage on Saturday, when, though I had to get up with the lark to hear the energetic old Eucken[101] lecture at 7 a.m., I had no lecture after 10, and went straight off to Weimar. I spent the rest of the morning (actually) in the museum, inspecting chiefly Preller's wall-paintings of the *Odyssey*[102]. They are the best criticism of the book I have seen and gave me a new and more pleasant idea of Odysseus.

---

[101] Rudolf Christoph Eucken (1846-1926), a philosopher who advocated a spiritual basis for activism in the educational and social arenas. He lectured in New York at NYU in 1913. Sorley spent one summer at Jena where Eucken lectured. —BR

[102] A series of frescoes painted after 1861 by Friedrich Preller the Elder (1804-1878) for the ducal museum in Weimar. The artist had executed tempera paintings on the same theme in Leipzig as early as 1834. —BR

Weimar does not give the same impression of musty age as parts of Jena. It seems a flourishing well-watered town, and I should like very much to live there, chiefly for the sake of the park. The name "Park" puts one off, but it is really a beautiful place like a college garden on an extensive scale. After I had wandered about there very pleasantly for an hour or so, I noticed a statue in a prominent position above me. "Another Goethe," thought I; but I looked at it again, and it had not that look of self-confident self-conscious greatness that all the Goethes have. So I went up to it and recognised a countryman looking down from this height on Weimar, with one eye half-closed and an attitude of head expressing amused and tolerant but penetrating interest. It was certainly the first satisfactory representation of Shakespeare I have ever seen. It appears quite new, but I could not discover the sculptor's name[103]. The one-eye-half-closed trick was most effective; you thought "this is a very humorous kindly human gentleman" — then you went round to the other side and saw the open eye! (*8 May* 1914)

---

[103] The statue dates from 1904 and was designed by Berlin sculptor Otto Lessing (1846-1912).—BR

IV
GERMANY

In the evening I am generally to be found avoiding a certain insincere type of German student, who hunts me down ostensibly to "tie a bond of good-comradeship," but really to work up facts about what "England" thinks. Such people of undeveloped individuality tell me in return what *wir Deutschen*[104] think, in a touching national spirit, which would have charmed Plato. But they don't charm me. Indeed I see in them the very worst result of 1871.[105] They have no idea beyond the "State," and have put me off Socialism for the rest of my life. They are not the kind of people, as [the Irish R.M.] puts it, "you could borrow half-a-crown to get drunk with."[106] But such is only a small proportion and come from the north and west; they just show how Sedan[107] has ruined one type of German, for I'm sure the German nature is the nicest in the world, as far as it is not warped by the German Empire. I like their lack of reserve and self-consciousness, our two national virtues. They all write poetry and recite it with gusto to any three hours' old acquaintance. We all write poetry too in England, but we write it on the bedroom wash-stand and lock the bedroom door, and disclaim it vehemently in public. (*2 June* 1914)

The two great sins people impute to Germany are that she says that might is right and bullies the little dogs. But I don't think she means that might *qua* might is right, but that confidence of superiority is right, and by superiority she means spiritual superiority. She said to Belgium,[108] "We enlightened

---

[104] *wir Deutschen*. We Germans.—WRS
[105] *1871*. Unification of the German principalities into one German nation, under the iron fist of Prussia. —BR
[106] *Borrow half a crown to get drunk with.* Sorley apparently encountered this expression in one of the three Irish novels by E. Somerville and M. Ross published between 1899 and 1915. I found a much earlier instance in Robert Smith Surtees' 1847 novel-memoir of the sporting life, *Jorrocks' Jaunts and Jollities.*—BR
[107] At the Battle of Sedan in 1870, the Prussians scored a crushing victory over the French and captured Napoleon III, ending the Franco-Prussian War and securing Germany's dominance in Europe. —BR

thinkers see that it is necessary to the world that all opposition to *Deutsche Kultur* should be crushed. As citizens of the world you must assist us in our object and assert those higher ideas of world-citizenship which are not bound by treaties. But if you oppose us, we have only one alternative." That, at least, is what the best of them would have said; only the diplomats put it rather more brusquely. She was going on a missionary voyage with all the zest of Faust —

> Er wandle so den Erdentag entlang;
> Wenn Geister spuken, geh' er seinen Gang;
> Im Weiterschreiten find' er Qual und Glück,
> Er, unbefriedigt jeden Augenblick!109

— and missionaries know no law ....

So it seems to me that Germany's only fault (and I think you often commented on it in those you met) is a lack of real insight and sympathy with those who differ from her. We are not fighting a bully, but a bigot. They are a young nation and don't yet see that what they consider is being done for the good of the world may be really being done for self-gratification — like X. who, under pretence of informing the form110 — dropped into the habit of parading his own knowledge. X. incidentally did the form a service by creating great amusement for it, and so is Germany incidentally doing the world a service (though not in the way it meant) by giving them something to live and die for, which no country but Germany had before. If the bigot conquers he will learn in time his mistaken methods (for it is only of the methods and not of the goal of Germany that one can disapprove) — just as the early Christian bigots conquered by bigotry and grew larger in sympathy and tolerance after conquest. I regard the war as one between sisters, between Martha and Mary, the efficient and intolerant against the casual and sympathetic. Each side has a virtue for which it is

---

108 German troops overran Belgium on August 3, 1914.—BR.
109 So let him journey through his earthly day,
Mid hustling spirits, go his self-found way,
Find torture, bliss, in every forward stride,
He, every moment still unsatisfied. —*Faust,* II, 6820-3. —WRS
110 *Form.* British equivalent to U.S. school "grades," numbered from one to six. —BR

fighting, and each that virtue's supplementary vice. And I hope that whatever the material result of the conflict, it will purge these two virtues of their vices, and efficiency and tolerance will no longer be incompatible.

But I think that tolerance is the larger virtue of the two, and efficiency must be her servant. So I am quite glad to fight against this rebellious servant. In fact I look at it this way. Suppose my platoon were the world. Then my platoon sergeant would represent efficiency and I would represent tolerance. And I always take the sternest measures to keep my platoon sergeant in check! I fully appreciate the wisdom of the War Office when they put inefficient officers to rule sergeants. *Adsit omen*.[111]

Now you know what Sorley thinks about it. And do excuse all his gassing. I know I already overdosed you on those five splendid days between Coblenz and Neumagen. But I've seen the Fatherland (I like to call it the Fatherland, for in many families Papa represents efficiency and Mamma tolerance — but don't think I'm W.S.P.U.)[112] so horribly misrepresented that I've been burning to put in my case for them to a sympathetic ear. *Wir sind gewiss Hamburger Jungen,* as that *lieber besoffener Osterreicher* told us[113] —. And so we must stand up for them, even while trying to knock them down. (*October* 1914)

On return to England, by the way, I renewed my acquaintance with Robert Browning. The last line of *Mr Sludge the Medium*[114] — "yet there is something in it, tricks and all" — converted me, and since then I have used no other. I wish we could recall him from the stars and get him to write a Dramatic Idyll or something, giving a soliloquy of the feelings and

---

[111] *Adsit omen.* Latin: May this be an omen.—BR
[112] *W.S.P.U.* Women's Social and Political Union, a leading women's suffrage organization. Women could not vote in Britain at all until 1918, when women over 30 who were householders were enfranchised. It took until 1928 for full female suffrage.—BR
[113] To be sure we are Hamburg lads, as that dear old tipsy Austrian told us.—WRS
[114] These lines from Browning's long poetic monologue, *Mr. Sludge the Medium,* "This trade of mine—I don't know, can't be sure/ But there was something in it, tricks and all" occur near the middle of the poem, not at the end. Sorley may have seen a shorter version of the poem. —BR

motives and quick changes of heat and cold that must be going through the poor Kaiser's mind at present. He would really show that impartial sympathy for him, which the British press and public so doltishly deny him, when in talk and comment they deny him even the rights of a human being. R. B. could do it perfectly — or Shakespeare.

I think the Kaiser not unlike Macbeth, with the military clique in Prussia as his Lady Macbeth, and the court flatterers as the three weird sisters. He'll be a splendid field for dramatists and writers in days to come. (*October* 1914)

It [a magazine article] brought back to me that little crooked old fellow that H. and I met at the fag-end of our hot day's walk as we swung into Neumagen.[115] His little face was lit with a wild uncertain excitement he had not known since 1870,[116] and he advanced towards us waving his stick and yelling at us *"Der Krieg ist los, Junge,"*[117] just as we might be running to watch a football match and he was come to tell us we must hurry up for the game had begun. And then the next night on the platform at Trier, train after train passing crowded with soldiers bound for Metz[118] — varied once or twice by a truck-load of "swarthier alien crews,"[119] thin old women like wineskins, with beautiful and piercing faces, and big heavy men and tiny aged-looking children: Italian colonists exiled to their country again.[120] Occasionally one of the men would jump out to fetch a glass of water to relieve their thirst in all that heat and crowding. The heat of the night is worse

---

[115] *Neumagen.* A wine-making village along the Moselle River, about 20 km from Trier. —BR.

[116] *1870.* The Franco-Prussian War.—BR

[117] "The war's begun, lad."—WRS

[118] *Metz.* Major fortified city in German-occupied Lorraine. The Germans had renamed the province "Lothringen" after annexing it at the end of the Franco-Prussian War. The inhabitants of French Alsace (renamed Elsass) and Lorraine/Lothringen speak German, which enhanced Germany's claim to the two provinces.—BR

[119] *Swarthier alien crews.* From Tennyson's poem, "The Revenge." —BR

[120] Despite its membership in the Triple Alliance, Italy refused to join Austria and Germany in commencing the war in August 1914. The ejection of guest-worker or immigrant Italians Sorley describes shows how quickly Germany retaliated. The following year, Italy, tempted by the prospect of gaining some Austrian territory, joined the war on the opposing side. —BR

than the heat of the day, and *geistige Getranke* were *verboten*.[121] Then the train would slowly move out into the darkness that led to Metz and an exact reproduction of it would stream in and fill its place: and we watched the signal on the southward side of Trier, till the lights should give a jump and the finger drop and let in the train which was to carry us out of that highly-strung and thrilling land.

At Cologne I saw a herd of some thirty American schoolmarms whom I had assisted to entertain at Eucken's[122] just a fortnight before. I shouted out to them, but they were far too upset to take any notice, but went bobbing into one compartment and out again and into another like people in a cinematograph. Their haste, anxiety and topsyturviness were caused by thoughts of their own safety and escape, and though perfectly natural contrasted so strangely with all the many other signs of haste, perturbation and distress that I had seen, which were much quieter and stronger and more full-bodied than that of those Americans, because it was the *Vaterland* and not the individual that was darting about and looking for the way and was in need: and the silent submissive unquestioning faces of the dark uprooted Italians peering from the squeaking trucks formed a fitting background — Cassandra from the backmost car looking steadily down on Agamemnon as he stepped from his triumphal purple chariot and Clytemnestra offered him her hand.[123] *(23 November 1914)*

It is surprising how very little difference a total change of circumstances and prospects makes in the individual. The German (I know from the 48 hours of the war that I spent there) is radically changed, and until he is sent to the front, his one dream and thought will be how quickest to die for his country. He is able more clearly to see the tremendous issues, and changes accordingly. I don't know whether it is because the English are more phlegmatic or more shortsighted or more egoistic or what, that makes them inwardly and outwardly so

---

[121] Spirituous drinks were forbidden —WRS

[122] *Eucken's*. Prof. Rudolf Christoph Eucken, whose lectures Sorley attended at Jena University.—BR

[123] *Cassandra and Agamemnon*. Refers to the central scene in Aeschylus's drama *Agamemnon* (458 BCE). Cassandra foresees that Agamemnon's wife and her lover will murder the King the moment he enters his palace.

far less shaken by the war than at first seemed probable. The German, I am sure, during the period of training "dies daily"[124] until he is allowed to die. We go there with our eyes shut. *(28 November* 1914*)*

We had a very swinging Christmas — one that makes one realize (in common with other incidents of the war) how near savages we are and how much the stomach (which Nietzsche calls the Father of Melancholy)[125] is also the best procurer of enjoyment. We gave the men a good church (plenty of loud hymns), a good dinner (plenty of beer), and the rest of the day was spent in sleep. I saw then very clearly that whereas for the upper classes Christmas is a spiritual debauch in which one remembers for a day to be generous and cheerful and open-handed, it is only a more or less physical debauch for the poorer classes, who need no reminder, since they are generous and cheerful and open-handed all the year round. One has fairly good chances of observing the life of the barrack-room, and what a contrast to the life of a house in a public school! The system is roughly the same: the house-master or platoon-commander entrusts the discipline of his charge to prefects or corporals, as the case may be. They never open their mouths in the barrack-room without the introduction of the unprintable swear-words and epithets: they have absolutely no "morality" (in the narrower, generally accepted sense): yet the public school boy should live among them to learn a little Christianity: for they are so extraordinarily nice to one another. They live in and for the present: we in and for the future. So they are cheerful and charitable always: and we often niggardly and unkind and spiteful. In the gymnasium at Marlborough, how the few clumsy specimens are ragged and despised and jeered at by the rest of the squad; in the gymnasium here you should hear the sounding cheer given to the man who has tried for eight weeks to make a long-jump of eight feet and at last by the advice and assistance of others has succeeded. They seem instinctively to regard a man singly, at his own rate, by his own standards and possibilities, not in

---

[124] *Dies daily.* From 1 *Corinthians* 15:31. —BR
[125] *Nietzsche.* In his autobiography, *Ecce Homo.* —BR

comparison with themselves or others: that's why they are so far ahead of us in their treatment and sizing up of others.

It's very interesting, what you say about Athens and Sparta, and England and Germany. Curious, isn't it, that in old days a nation fought another for land or money: now we are fighting Germany for her spiritual qualities — thoroughness, and fearlessness of effort, and effacement of the individual. I think that Germany, in spite of her vast bigotry and blindness, is in a kind of way living up to the motto that Goethe left her in the closing words of *Faust,* before he died.

> Ay, in this thought is my whole life's persistence,
> This is the whole conclusion of the true:
> He only earns his Freedom, owns Existence,
> Who every day must conquer her anew!
> So let him journey through his earthly day,
> Mid hustling spirits, go his self-found way,
> Find torture, bliss, in every forward stride,
> He, every moment still unsatisfied.[126]

A very close parallel may be drawn between Faust and present history (with Belgium as Gretchen).[127] And Faust found spiritual salvation in the end! (*27 December* 1914)

---

[126] *Faust,* II, 6944-7, 6820-3. —WRS
[127] *Gretchen.* Gretchen is the innocent girl whom Faust seduces and destroys.

V
MANY A BETTER ONE (p. 79)

———'s death was a shock. Still, since Achilles' *katthane kai Patroklos o per seo pollon ameinon,*[128] which should be read at the grave of every corpse in addition to the burial service, no saner and splendider comment on death has been made, especially, as here, where it seemed a cruel waste. (*28 November* 1914)

---

[128] *katthane kai Patroklos* ... Died Patroclus too who was a far better man than thou. — *Iliad,* xxi, 107— WRS.

VI
"BLANK SUMMER'S SURFEIT" (p. 80)

From the time that the May blossom is scattered till the first frosts of September, one is always at one's worst. Summer is stagnating: there is no more spring (in both senses) anywhere. When the corn is grown and the autumn seed not yet sown, it has only to bask in the sun, to fatten and ripen: a damnable time for man, heaven for the vegetables. And so I am sunk deep in *Denkfaulheit*,[129] trying to catch in the distant but incessant upper thunder of the air promise of October rainstorms: long runs clad only in jersey and shorts over the Marlborough downs, cloked[130] in rain, as of yore: likewise, in the aimless toothless grumbling of the guns, promise of a great advance to come: hailstones and coals of fire. (*July* 1915)

---

[129] *Denkfaultheit*. Mental lethargy —WRS
[130] *Cloke*. Variant of "cloak." —BR

VII
"ETERNALLY TO DO" (p. 81)

Masefield[131] has founded a new school of poetry and given a strange example to future poets; and this is wherein his greatness and originality lies: that he is a man of action not imagination. For he has one of the fundamental qualities of a great poet — a thorough enjoyment of life. He has it in a more pre-eminent degree than even Browning, perhaps the stock instance of a poet who was great because he liked life. Everyone has read the latter's lines about "the wild joys of living, the leaping from rock up to rock."[132] These are splendid lines: but one somehow does not feel that Browning ever leapt from rock up to rock himself. He saw other people doing it, doubtless, and thought it fine. But I don't think he did it himself ever. . . .

Masefield writes that he knows and testifies that he has seen. Throughout his poems there are lines and phrases so instinct with life, that they betoken a man who writes of what he has experienced, not of what he thinks he can imagine: who has braved the storm, who has walked in the hells, who has seen the reality of life: who does not, like Tennyson, shut off the world he has to write about, attempting to imagine shipwrecks from the sofa, or battles in his bed. Compare for instance *Enoch Arden*[133] and *Dauber.*[134] One is a dream: the other, life ....

The sower, who reaps not, has found a voice at last — a harsh rough voice, compelling, strong, triumphant. Let us, the reapers where we have not sown, give ear to it. Are they not much better than we? The voice of our poets and men of letters is finely trained and sweet to hear; it teems with sharp saws

---

[131] John Masefield (1878-1967), noted for sea poetry and narrative poems, was British Poet Laureate from 1930 to 1967. —BR
[132] *The wild joys of living* ... From Robert Browning's poem," Saul." —BR
[133] *Enoch Arden*. An 1864 Tennyson poem about a ship captain returning home after a long absence to find his wife remarried. Unlike Odysseus, Enoch Arden chooses not to reveal his identity. —BR
[134] *Dauber*. A 1912 narrative poem by Masefield, on the career and death of a young sailor-painter, includes hair-raising storms and a realistic portrayal of shipboard life. —BR

and rich sentiment: it is a marvel of delicate technique: it pleases, it flatters, it charms, it soothes: it is a living lie. The voice of John Masefield rings rough and ill trained: it tells a story, it leaves the thinking to the reader, it gives him no dessert of sentiment, cut, dried, — and ready made to go to sleep on: it jars, it grates, it makes him wonder; it is full of hope and faith and power and strife and God. Till Mr. Masefield came on earth, the poetry of the world had been written by the men who lounged, who looked on. It is sin in a man to write of the world before he has known the world, and the failing of every poet up till now has been that he has written of what he loved to imagine but dared not to experience. But Masefield writes that he knows and testifies that he has seen; with him expression is the fruit of action, the sweat of a body that has passed through the fire.

We stand by the watershed of English poetry; for the vastness and wonder of modern life has demanded that men should know what they write about. Behind us are the poets of imagination; before us are the poets of fact. For Masefield as a poet may be bad or good: I think him good, but you may think him bad: but, good or bad, he has got this quality which no one can deny and few belittle. He is the first of a multitude of coming poets (so I trust and pray) who are men of action before they are men of speech and men of speech because they are men of action. Those whom, because they do not live in our narrow painted groove, we call the Lower Classes, it is they who truly know what life is: so to them let us look for the true expression of life. One has already arisen, and his name is Masefield. We await the coming of others in his train. (Essay on Masefield, *3 November* 1912)

The war is a chasm in time.... In a job like this, one lives in times a year ago — and a year hence, alternately. *Keine Nachricht.*[135] A large amount of organized disorderliness, killing the spirit. A vagueness and a dullness everywhere: an unromantic sitting still 100 yards from Brother Bosch.[136]

---

[135] *Keine Nachricht.* No news. — WRS
[136] *Bosch.* Usually spelled "Boche," a derogatory French nickname for Germans from "Tête de boche," meaning obstinate or pig-headed. British soldiers picked up the name from their French and Belgian comrades. Sorley's spelling may be a conflation with Hieronymous Bosch, the

There's something rotten in the state of something. One feels it but cannot be definite of what. Not even is there the premonition of something big impending: gathering and ready to burst. None of that feeling of confidence, offensiveness, "personal ascendancy," with which the reports so delight our people at home. Mutual helplessness and lassitude, as when two boxers who have battered each other crouch dancing two paces from each other, waiting for the other to hit. Improvised organization, with its red hat, has muddled out romance. It is not the strong god of the Germans — that makes their Prussian *Beamter*[137] so bloody and their fight against fearful odds so successful. Our organization is like a nasty fat old frowsy cook dressed up in her mistress's clothes: fussy, unpopular, and upstart: trailing the scent of the scullery behind her. In periods of rest we are billeted in a town of sewage farms, mean streets, and starving cats: delightful population: but an air of late June weariness. For Spring again! This is not Hell as I hoped, but Limbo Lake with green growths on the water, full of minnows.

So one lives in a year ago — and a year hence. What are your feet doing, a year hence? ... where, while riding in your Kentish lanes, are you riding twelve months hence? I am sometimes in Mexico, selling cloth: or in Russia, doing Lord knows what: in Serbia or the Balkans: in England, never. England remains the dream, the background: at once the memory and the ideal. Sorley is the Gaelic for wanderer. I have had a conventional education: Oxford would have corked it. But this has freed the spirit, glory be. Give me the *Odyssey,* and I return the New Testament to store. Physically as well as spiritually, give me the road.

Only sometimes the horrible question of bread and butter shadows the dream: it has shadowed many, I should think. It must be tackled. But I always seek to avoid the awkward, by postponing it.

You figure in these dreams as the pioneer-sergeant. Perhaps *you* are the Odysseus, I am but one of the dog-like

---

painter, or a case of transcribing/Germanizing a word he had heard but not seen in print. —BR

[137] *Beamter.* German: Official. —WRS

hetairoi[138]... But however that may be, our lives will be *polyplanktoi*,[139] though our paths may be different. And we will be buried by the sea —

> Timon will make his everlasting mansion
> Upon the beachèd verge of a salt flood,
> Which twice a day with his embossèd froth
> The turbulent surge shall cover. [140]

Details can wait — perhaps for ever. These are the plans. (*16 June* 1915)

---

[138] *hetairoi*. Greek: comrades —WRS
[139] *polyplanktoi*. Greek: far-roaming —WRS
[140] *Timon will make...* From the last scene of Shakespeare's *Timon of Athens*. Sorley alters the tense to future to suit his purpose. The original reads:

> Come not to me again: but say to Athens,
> Timon hath made his everlasting mansion
> Upon the beached verge of the salt flood;
> Who once a day with his embossed froth
> The turbulent surge shall cover: thither come,
> And let my grave-stone be your oracle.
> Lips, let sour words go by and language end:
> What is amiss plague and infection mend!
> Graves only be men's works and death their gain!
> Sun, hide thy beams! Timon hath done his reign. —BR

VIII
"THE GRANDEUR OF THEIR MESS" (p. 83)

I am bleached with chalk and grown hairy. And I think exultantly and sweetly of the one or two or three outstandingly admirable meals of my life. One in Yorkshire, in an inn upon the moors, with a fire of logs and ale and tea and every sort of Yorkshire bakery, especially bears me company. And yet another in Mecklenburg-Schwerin (where they are very English) in a farm-house utterly at peace in broad fields sloping to the sea. I remember a tureen of champagne in the middle of the table to which we helped ourselves with ladles! I remember my hunger after three hours' ride over the country: and the fishing-town of Wismar lying like an English town on the sea. In that great old farm-house where I dined at 3 p.m. as the May day began to cool, fruit of sea and of land joined hands together, fish fresh caught and ducks fresh killed: it was a wedding of the elements. It was perhaps the greatest meal I have had ever, for everything we ate had been alive that morning — the champagne was alive yet. We feasted like kings till the sun sank, for it was impossible to overeat. 'Twas Homeric and its memory fills many hungry hours. *(5 October 1915)*

IX
"THE OLD WAR-JOY, THE OLD WAR-PAIN" (p. 84)

This is a little hamlet, smelling pleasantly of manure. I have never felt more restful. We arrived at dawn: white dawn across the plane trees and coming through the fields of rye. After two hours in an oily ship and ten in a grimy train, the "war area" was a haven of relief. These French trains shriek so: there is no sight more desolating than abandoned engines passing up and down the lines, hooting in their loneliness. There is something eerie in a railway by night.

But this is perfect. The other officers have heard the heavy guns and perhaps I shall soon. They make perfect cider in this valley: still, like them. There are clouds of dust along the roads, and in the leaves: but the dust here is native and caressing and pure, not like the dust of Aldershot,[141] gritted and fouled by motors and thousands of feet. 'Tis a very Limbo lake: set between the tireless railways behind and twenty miles in front the fighting. Drink its cider and paddle in its rushy streams: and see if you care whether you die tomorrow. It brings out a new part of oneself, the loiterer, neither scorning nor desiring delights, gliding listlessly through the minutes from meal-time to meal-time, like the stream through the rushes: or stagnant and smooth like their cider, unfathomably gold: beautiful and calm without mental fear. And in four-score hours we will pull up our braces and fight. These hours will have slipt over me, and I shall march hotly to the firing-line, by turn critic, actor, hero, coward, and soldier of fortune: perhaps even for a moment Christian, humble, with "Thy will be done." Then shock, combustion, the emergence of one of these: death or life: and then return to the old rigmarole. I imagine that this, while it may or may not knock about your body, will make very little difference to you otherwise.

A speedy relief from Chatham. There is vibration in the air when you hear "The Battalion will move across the water on. . . ."

---

141 *Aldershot*. Southwest of London, England's largest military base. — BR

The moon won't rise till late, but there is such placid weariness in all the bearing earth, that I must go out to see. I have not been *auf dem Lande*[142] for many years: *man muss den Augenblick geniessen.*[143] (*1 June* 1915)

Your letter arrived and awoke the now drifting ME to consciousness. I had understood and acquiesced in your silence. The re-creation of that self which one is to a friend is an effort: repaying if it succeeds, but not to be forced. Wherefore, were it not for the dangers dancing attendance on the adjourning type of mind — which a year's military training has not been able to efface from me — I should not be writing to you now. For it is just after breakfast — and you know what breakfast is: putter-to-sleep of all mental energy and discontent: charmer, sedative, leveler: maker of Britons. I should wait till after tea when the undiscriminating sun has shown his back — a fine back — on the world, and oneself by the aid of tea has thrown off the mental sleep of heat. But after tea I am on duty. So with bacon in my throat and my brain like a poached egg I will try to do you justice. . . .

I wonder how long it takes the King's Pawn, who so proudly initiates the game of chess, to realize that he is a pawn. Same with us. We are finding out that we play the unimportant if necessary part. At present a dam, untested, whose presence not whose action stops the stream from approaching: and then — a mere handle to steel: dealers of death which we are not allowed to plan. But I have complained enough before of the minion state of the "damned foot." It is something to have no responsibility — an inglorious ease of mind . . .

Health — and I don't know what ill-health is — invites you so much to smooth and shallow ways: where a happiness may only be found by renouncing the other happiness of which one set out in search. Yet here there is enough to stay the bubbling surface stream. Looking into the future one sees a holocaust somewhere: and at present there is — thank God — enough of "experience" to keep the wits edged (a callous way of putting it, perhaps).

---

[142] *Auf dem Lande.* In the country . —WRS
[143] *man muss den Augenblick geniessen.* One must enjoy the passing moment . —WRS

But out in front at night in that no-man's land and long graveyard there is a freedom and a spur. Rustling of the grasses and grave tap-tapping of distant workers: the tension and silence of encounter, when one struggles in the dark for moral victory over the enemy patrol: the wail of the exploded bomb and the animal cries of wounded men. Then death and the horrible thankfulness when one sees that the next man is dead: "We won't have to carry him in under fire, thank God; dragging will do": hauling in of the great resistless body in the dark: the smashed head rattling: the relief, the relief that the thing has ceased to groan: that the bullet or bomb that made the man an animal has now made the animal a corpse. One is hardened by now: purged of all false pity: perhaps more selfish than before. The spiritual and the animal get so much more sharply divided in hours of encounter, taking possession of the body by swift turns. (*26 August* 1915)

The chess players are no longer waiting so infernal long between their moves. And the patient pawns are all in movement, hourly expecting further advances — whether to be taken or reach the back lines and be queened. 'Tis sweet, this pawn-being: there are no cares, no doubts: wherefore no regrets. The burden which I am sure is the parent of ill-temper drunkenness and premature old age — to wit, the making up of one's own mind — is lifted from our shoulders. I can now understand the value of dogma, which is the General Commander-in-chief of the mind. I am now beginning to think that free thinkers should give their minds into subjection, for we who have given our actions and volitions into subjection gain such marvelous rest thereby. Only of course it is the subjecting of their powers of will and deed to a wrong master on the part of a great nation that has led Europe into war. Perhaps afterwards I and my likes will again become indiscriminate rebels. For the present we find high relief in making ourselves soldiers. *(5 October* 1915*)*

X
"PERHAPS THE ROAD UP ILSLEY WAY, THE OLD RIDGE-TRACK, WILL BE MY WAY"
(p. 84)

No! When I next come down to Marlborough it shall be an entry worthy of the place and of the enterer. Not in khaki, with gloves and a little cane, with creased trousers from Aldershot — "dyed garments from Bozrah"[144] — but in grey bags, an old coat and a knapsack, coming over the downland from Chiseldon, putting up at the Sun![145] Then after a night there and a tattered stroll through the High Street, feeling perhaps the minor inconveniences of complete communion with Nature, I should put on a gentlemanly suit and crave admittance at your door, talk old scandal, search old House-books, swank in Court and sing in Chapel and be a regular O.M.: retaining always the right on Monday afternoon (it always rains on Mondays in Marlborough) to sweat[146] round Barbury and Totterdown, what time you dealt out nasty little oblong unseens[147] to the Upper VI. This would be my Odyssey. At present I am too cornered by my uniform for any such luxuries. *(May* 1915*)*

There is really very little to say about the life here. Change of circumstance, I find, means little compared to change of company. And as one has gone out and is still with the same officers with whom one had rubbed shoulders unceasingly for the last nine months, and of whom one had acquired that extraordinarily intimate knowledge which comes of constant *synousia*[148]*,* one does not notice the change: until one or two or three drop off. And one wonders why.

---

[144] *Dyed garments from Bozrah* ... From *Isaiah* 63:1 "Who is this that cometh from Edom, with dyed garments from Bozrah? this that is glorious in his apparel, travelling in the greatness of his strength?" —BR

[145] The Sun Inn in Marlborough, dating to the 15th century. —BR

[146] *Sweat.* Run. —BR

[147] *Unseens.* Material for translation, not previously seen or worked on by the students.

[148] *synousia.* Greek. Companionship. — WRS

They are extraordinarily close, really, these friendships of circumstance, distinct as they remain from friendships of choice.... Only, I think, once or twice does one stumble across that person into whom one fits at once: to whom one can stand naked, all disclosed. But circumstance provides the second best: and I'm sure that any gathering of men will in time lead to a very very close half-friendship between them all (I only say half-friendship because I wish to distinguish it from the other).

So there has really been no change in coming over here: the change is to come when half of this improvised "band of brothers"[149] are wiped away in a day. We are learning to be soldiers slowly — that is to say, adopting the soldierly attitude of complete disconnection with our job during odd hours. No shop. So when I think I should tell you "something about the trenches," I find I have neither the inclination nor the power.

This however. On our weekly march from the trenches back to our old farmhouse a mile or two behind, we leave the communication-trench for a road, hedged on one side only, with open ploughland to the right. It runs a little down hill till the road branches. Then half left up over open country goes our track, with the ground shelving away to the right of us. Can you see it? The Toll House to the First Post on Trainers Down on a small scale. There is something in the way that at the end of the hedge the road leaps up to the left into the beyond that puts me in mind of Trainers Down. It is what that turn into unhedged country and that leap promises, not what it achieves, that makes the likeness. It is nothing when you get up, no wildness, no openness. But there it remains to cheer me on each relief....

---

[149] Band of brothers. "We few, we happy few, we band of brothers" from Shakespeare's *Henry V*, IV:iii

I hear that a *very* select group of public schools will by this time be enjoying the Camp "somewhere in England." May they not take it too seriously! Seein' as 'ow all training is washed out as soon as you turn that narrow street corner at Boulogne,150 where some watcher with a lantern is always up for the English troops arriving, with a "Bon courage" for every man.

A year ago to-day — but that way madness lies. (*4 August 1915*)

---

150 *Boulogne*. Seaport on the NW coast of France which served as the major supply port for Britain during the War. It was also the site of major hospitals for battle casualties. A soldier — if he was lucky — saw Boulogne twice: once on arriving and once when sent home with injuries sufficient to keep him from returning to the Front again. —BR

XI
SORLEY AS TRANSLATOR

The lines translated from *Faust* [on page 108] are almost the only example of verse translation by the author. Another specimen, which was found in a school note-book, is a rendering of Horace, *Odes,* I, 24. It is not likely that he would have printed it himself, but it is quoted here as an epilogue to these notes. — WRS.

QUIS DESIDERIO

Check not thy tears, nor be ashamed to sorrow
For one so dear. Sing us a plaintive song.
O Muse, who from thy sire the lute didst borrow
The lute and notes melodious and strong.
So will he wake again from slumber never?
O, when will Purity, to Justice dear,
Faith unalloyed and Truth unspotted ever,
When will these virtues ever find his peer?
For him the tears of noble men are flowing,
But thine, O Virgil, bitterest of all!
Thou prayest God to give him back, not knowing
He may not, cannot hearken to thy call.

For if thy lyre could move the forests, swelling
More sweetly than the Thracian bard's of old,
His soul could not revisit its old dwelling;
For now among the dead he is enrolled
By Mercury, all deaf to supplication,
Obdurate, gathering all with ruthless rod.
'Tis hard; but Patience lightens Tribulation
When to remove it is denied by God.

CRITICISM AND SORLEIANA

CHARLES HAMILTON SORLEY:
AN ANNOTATED CHECKLIST (1915-1973)

by LARRY K. UFFELMAN

In 1915, at the age of twenty, Charles Hamilton Sorley was killed by a sniper's bullet. His poetry was subsequently collected and published by his father, the last edition appearing in 1932. As one of the early "war poets," he has achieved a place in literary history and has maintained a small but admiring audience.

The best text of Sorley's poems remains the Miscellany edition of *Marlborough and Other Poems* published by the Cambridge University Press in 1932. This edition was intended by W. R. Sorley, the poet's father and only editor, to be "definitive." As such, it contains a biographical note, the poems themselves, and a considerable body of notes with cross references to the poet's letters wherever appropriate. In 1916, the poet's family privately published at the Cambridge University Press C.H.S.'s *Letters from Germany*, a collection they had made from those letters written while Charles was in Schwerin studying German and later while he was a student at the University of Jena. Because of the interest aroused by this volume, the family published *The Letters of Charles Sorley, with a Chapter of Biography* (London: Cambridge University Press, 1919). This collection incorporates *Letters from Germany*, and its "Chapter of Biography," written by Mrs. Sorley, remains a principal source of personal information about the poet.

With the publication of John H. Johnston's *English Poetry of the First World War* (1964), Bernard Bergonzi's *Heroes" Twilight* (1965), and Thomas B. Swann's *The Ungirt Runner: Charles Hamilton Sorley, Poet of World War I* (1965), Charles Sorley's life and poetic achievement underwent re-examination. Far from diminishing his reputation, these studies considerably enhanced it.

Believing that such a Sorley "revival" justifies a listing of items about the poet, I have made this compilation. The checklist is not complete. It does not record every mention of Charles Sorley, nor does it cite all histories of English literature. Likewise, it does not record all of the anthologies in which Sorley's work appears. Instead, I have attempted to include all articles and books which, by making a qualitative statement about his work, place Sorley in a historical context. Thus, a few representative literary histories appear, as well as a few anthologies — but only those anthologies whose editors comment critically on the poet's work. . . .Because I saw the newspaper reviews of Sorley's work in scrapbook form in the collection of Mr. Kenneth Sorley, page references to several reviews were not available. I hope that I have not missed anything of major importance.

By far the pleasantest aspect of compiling a checklist such as mine is the opportunity it provides for publicly thanking many gracious people for their help. I wish to acknowledge the considerable assistance of the following libraries and their staffs: Cornell University Library, the Arizona State University Library, the University of Illinois Library, the Manchester (England) Public Library and particularly the assistance of Miss Catherine Reilly, and the Mansfield State College Library, and particularly the assistance of Mrs. Winil Borg and Miss Jean Horning. For their continued interest and aid, I wish to thank members of the Sorley family, Mr. and Mrs. Kenneth Sorley and Professor and Mrs. Geoffrey L. Bickersteth. Thanks are also due to Mansfield State College for allowing me time to work on this project. However, a special word must be reserved for the faculty of Marlborough College, Marlborough, Wiltshire, and particularly for Mr. Gerald W. Murray, College librarian, for kindnesses too numerous to detail.

Poems First Published in *The Marlburian*
"Verses for a C1 House Concert," July 29, 1912.
"A Tale of Two Careers," Nov. 11, 1912.
"A Call to Action," Nov. 21, 1912.
"Rain," Nov. 21, 1912.
"Peace," Dec. 19, 1912.
"The River," Feb. 25, 1913.
"The Seekers," March 13, 1913.
"What You Will," July 10, 1913.
"Rooks I," July 28, 1913.
"Rooks II," July 28, 1913.
"Stones," July 28, 1913.
"Autumn Dawn," Oct. 9, 1913.
"J. B.," Oct. 9, 1913.
"Richard Jefferies," Oct. 9, 1913.
"East Kennet Church at Evening," Dec. 3, 1913.
"The Other Wise Man," Feb. 10, 1914.
"Return," March 3, 1914.
"Expectans Expectavi," Nov. 24, 1915.
"In Memoriam, S. C. W., V. C.," Nov. 24, 1915.
"Two Sonnets," Nov. 24, 1915.

Biography and Criticism
Adcock, Arthur St. John. "For Remembrance: Soldier-Poets Who Have Fallen in the War." *Bookman* (London), 53 (December 1917, Christmas Supplement), 70-91. (C.H.S.'s "All the Hills and Vales Along" shows what a "little thing he could make of the death he was to die." This attitude also dominates Grenfell's "Into Battle" and Brooke's "If I should die think only this of me."]

———. *For Remembrance: Soldier-Poets Who Have Fallen in the War*. London: Hodder and Stoughton, 1920. [C.H.S.'s "All the Hills and Vales Along" shows what a "little thing he could make of the death he was to die." Sorley conveys a sense of "mystical joy in dying for a great end" which links him to Brooke, Grenfell, and J. W. Streets.]

Allen, Walter. "A Literary Aftermath." *Promise of Greatness: The War of 1914-1918*. Ed. George A. Panichas. Foreword by Sir Herbert Read. New York: The John Day Co., 1968. [For poets such as Owen, Rosenberg, and Sorley, "no recollection of emotion in tranquillity was possible; they wrote ... in the white heat of experience itself." Sorley's poetry and letters reveal "an astonishingly tough and mature mind."]

Altick, Richard D. "The Sociology of Authorship: The Social Origins, Education, and Occupations of 1,110 British Writers, 1800-1935." *Bulletin of the New York Public Library*, 66 (1962), 389-404. [Altick does not mention Sorley by name; however, he includes statistics on the literary men of Marlborough College.]

Beeching, H. C. "English War Poetry: A Lecture." *Norwich Public Library Readers' Guide*, 7 (April 1918), 19-28. [C.H.S.'s two sonnets on death are typical of war poetry in that they prefer deeds to words and are responsive to "a few great words like Duty, and Honour, and Freedom .... "]

Bergonzi, Bernard. *Heroes' Twilight: A Study of the Literature of the Great War*. New York: Coward-McCann, Inc., 1965; American edition, 1966. [Sorley's letters convey the "essential quality of his mind" in ways reminiscent of the great letter writers in English. His maturity and often ironic detachment also appear in his best poetry. The war hurried his poetic development "towards the full artistic maturity that he had not altogether reached at the time of his death." The result is that his poetry about the war is complex, "lacking the single-mindedness of Brooke or Grenfell." C.H.S.'s early death was a tragedy for English letters.]

Blunden, Edmund. *War Poets, 1914-1918*. London: Longmans, Green and Co., Writers and Their Work No. 100, 1958. [Sorley knew from experience what Brooke would have known if he had lived longer. At twenty years of age, Sorley "was a thinker and a writer capable of illuminating matters of permanent importance, alike in verse and prose."]

Brereton, Frederick [pseud. for Frederick Thomas Smith], ed. *An Anthology of War Poems*. Introduction by Edmund Blunden. London: V. Collins and Sons, 1930. [Like Rupert Brooke, Sorley did not live to know the full horror of the war. However, he began to sense the futility of the war and the alienation of the men at the front from the people at home.]

Bullough, Geoffrey. "The War Poetry of Two Wars." *Cairo Studies in English* (1959), 43-58. [The attitude toward war voiced by Rupert Brooke, the chivalric view that war provided "a positive opportunity for him and his like to shape themselves into full manhood," appears in the work of Sorley, William N. Hodgson, and Julian Grenfell.]

Burns, Vincent Godfrey, ed. *The Red Harvest: A Cry for Peace.* New York: The Macmillan Co., 1930. [British soldiers of World War I regarded the Germans as brothers. C.H.S.'s "To Germany" is evidence.]

Bush, Douglas. *Mythology and the Romantic Tradition in English Poetry.* New York: W. W. Norton Co., 1963. [Unexpectedly, "the reality of war" encouraged rather than banished "dreams of Hellas." In France, C. H. S. vividly recalled the *Odyssey*.]

Bushnell, Athalie. "Charles Hamilton Sorley." *The Poetry Review*, 36 (Nov.-Dec. 1945), 285-292. [The evidence of the published poems makes it unlikely that C.H.S. would have become a great poet. Several poems (e.g., "Le Revenant") show the influence of A.E. Housman; others exhibit the "finality and fatality" of Hardy and Meredith (*e.g.*, "All the Hills and Vales Along"). Had he lived, C.H.S. would have gone into some form of social work; "he would not, could not, have spent his life behind a desk, writing sonnets in an 'escapist' frame of mind."]

Butler, Lord R. A. "Charles Sorley." *The Marlburian* (Michaelmas Term, 1970). [Since the publication of Robert Nichols' anthology of war poetry in 1943, the memory of C.H.S. has faded. Still, "he remains one of the most promising young intellectual figures killed in action a few months after reaching France." The poems of Rosenberg and Owen are more finished, but "it cannot be sufficiently stressed" that they had "several years more ... in which to perfect their poetry." Had he lived, C.H.S. might well have gone into social work and then turned to drama. His loss was a certain deprivation.]

Caldwell, Thomas, ed. *The Golden Book of Modern English Poetry*, 1870-1930. Introduction by Lord Dunsany. Abridged edition. London: J. M. Dent and Sons, 1930. ["All the Hills and Vales Along" is a "fine marching song."]

Clark, George Herbert. *A Treasury of War Poetry: British and American Poems of the World War, 1914-1917.* New York: Houghton Mifflin Co., 1917; Second Series, 1918. [Series One: Sorley is one of the war poets whose insight is quickened in the face of death. Series Two: C.H.S.'s "To Germany" is an example of the fighting poet's reluctance to hate the enemy.]

Collins, A. S. *English Literature of the Twentieth Century.* London: University Tutorial Press, Ltd, Fourth edition, 1960. [C.H.S. was one of those soldiers who "made poetry out of war."]

Comfort, Alex. "English Poetry and the War." *Partisan Review*, 10 (March 1943), 191-195. [*Poems from the Forces*, an anthology of poetry by soldiers of World War II, lacks experience "of real war, such as Owen and Sorley knew."]

Dalglish, Doris. "Charles Sorley." *The Friends' Quarterly Examiner*, 71 (Oct. 1937) 346-359. [C.H.S.'s work will "endure" because the war "neither made nor liberated his poetry." His love of nature and the Marlborough downs makes him poetic kin to Richard Jefferies. The dominant mark of his verse is "austerity."]

Darton, F. J. Harvery. *From Surtees to Sassoon: Some English Contrasts (1838-1928)*. London: Morley and Mitchell Kennerley Jr., 1931. [C.H.S. and his comrades, where they are articulate, say the same thing —"that they have gone into the conflict to save Liberty and England. . . ."]

Das Gupta, N. *Literature of the Twentieth Century*. Gwalior 1: Kitab Ghar, 1967. [The real war poetry was written by Sorley, Sassoon, Rosenberg, and Owen. C.H.S. sees no aim or ideal in the war, and finds sacrifice meaningless. He is conscious too of the "limitations of narrow nationalism"; his work is the product of both intellect and experience.]

Dickinson, Patrie. "Poets of the First World War." *The Listener*, 67 (Feb. 8, 1962), 259-260. [Sorley would have agreed with Sassoon's letter of 1917 stating that the war had become aggressive instead of defensive. C.H.S. was "a poet of remarkable potentialities." His works "mark the end of a phase of war poetry and indeed of the war. Sorley, as a person, looks forward."]

——— "The 'Ungirt Runner.' " BBC Broadcast (Nov. 1959; repeated Dec. 1959). [Sorley was a fine poet. It is a pity he was killed.]

Earp, W. J. "Charles Sorley: An Assessment." *The Marlburian Literary: Supplement*, No. 3 (Christmas Term 1966). [The two dominant facets of Sorley's poetry are "his preoccupation with death, and his love of Marlborough and its characteristic wild weather." C.H.S. did not give in to "the sentimental heroics of Brooke and Grenfell," and he died before the war revealed its full horror. Prints corrections to and supplies missing lines of "I have not brought my Odyssey."]

Elton, Oliver. *The English Muse*. London: G. Bell and Sons, Ltd., 1933. [C.H.S.'s talent was revealed early in "Song of the Ungirt Runner" and "To Poets."]

Enright, D. J. "The Literature of the First World War," *The Modern Age*, Vol. 7 of *The Pelican Guide to English Literature*, ed. Boris Ford. Baltimore: Pelican Books, 1961. [Everything that Rupert Brooke said in his war poetry "was said, with far more authority" by poets such as C.H.S. Sorley was critical of Brooke's "sentimental attitudes"; he himself viewed the war as a conflict "of soldiers against politicians rather than nationality against nationality."]

Gardner, Brian, ed. *Up the Line to Death: The War Poets 1914-1918*. Foreword by Edmund Blunden. London: Methuen and Co., 1964. [Although some of the poems of the war are well remembered, those by C.H.S. are in danger of being forgotten. Sorley is not held in high opinion these days, but "John Masefield told [Robert] Nichols that Sorley was potentially the greatest poet lost in the war."]

Garratt, Vero W. "The War-Poetry of Soldier Poets." *English Review*, 33 (July 1921), 50-53. [The soldier-poets have presented warfare stripped of artificiality. In them there is no glorification of warfare or hate; " ... it is indeed refreshing to remember that at a time when the gospel of hate was being preached at its highest, Hamilton Sorley" had already written "To Germany."]

Gay, Frances J. "Charles Sorley's Poems." *The Swindon Review: A Local Miscellany of the Arts*, No.4 (Dec. 1948), 5-9. [It is fitting that Sorley's poem "Richard Jefferies" was given prominence at the Jefferies' Centenary Exhibition. C.H.S.'s love of Wiltshire and the downs are reflected by his admiration of Jefferies' poetry. But he was "no blind follower of Richard Jefferies." Sorley is "associated with aspects and features of Marlborough and its countryside ... ." Among these are "Sorley's Signpost" and Barbury.]

Goldring, Douglas. "The War and the Poets." *Reputations*. London: Chapman and Hall, 1920. [The kind of education provided by the Public Schools did not prepare their students for the realities of war. It is their ability to view the world only through tinted glasses that renders "the poems of so many young subalterns so valueless as literature, so tragic and accusing as human documents." War poets who had something to say include Alan Seeger and Wilfred Sorley [sic], both of whom "were moved at moments to sincerity."]

Gosse, Edmund William. *Some Diversions of a Man of Letters*. London: William Heineman, 1919. [C.H.S. "gave evidence of precocious literary talents," though perhaps more so in prose than verse. His verse lacks the "singing faculty."]

Grant, Joy. *Harold Munro and the Poetry Bookshop*. London: Routledge and Kegan Paul, 1967. [Post-war readings given by Munro and his wife included a session on the war poets. Presented were seven poems by C.H.S. and five by Wilfred Owen.]

Graves, Robert. *The Common Asphodel: Collected Essays on Poetry 1922-1949*. London: Hamish Hamilton, 1949. [C.H.S.'s criticism of Rupert Brooke exemplifies changing attitudes toward war. "Of the War Poets whose works were temporarily advertised by their death in action only three can be regretted as poets: Sorley, Rosenberg, and Owen."]

———. *Fairies and Fusiliers*. New York: Alfred A. Knopf, 1918. [Contains the poem "Sorley's Weather."]

———. *Good-Bye to All That*. London: Jonathan Cope, 1929. [Notes the death of Sorley.]

———. "Poets in War and Peace." *Saturday Review of Literature*, 1 (Nov. 1, 1924), 250. [Sorley is one of "several prominent younger poets who first began writing while soldiers, though saying little or nothing about the War." 'With Rosenberg and Owen, C.H.S. is one of the "least calculable losses to English poetry."]

Green, Walford D. "Ideals of the Soldier Poets." *London Quarterly Review*, 129 (April 1918), 215-225; reprinted, *The Living Age*, 297 (June 15, 1918), 671-677. [C.H.S. was "one of the earliest and most thoughtful of our soldier poets."]

Grieg, Nordahl. *De Unge Døde*: *Keats, Shelley, Byron; Brooke, Sorley, Owen*. Oslo, 1932. [C.H.S. is "one of the noblest figures of English literature."]

Grierson, Herbert J. C. and J. C. Smith. "Twentieth-Century Poetry: The War Years, 1914-1918." *A Critical History of English Poetry*. London: Chatto and Windus, 1950. [It is impossible to estimate the loss to English poetry by the death of C.H.S. and his contemporaries killed in the war. Sorley's *Marlborough and Other Poems* shows "extraordinary promise."]

Hamburger, Michael. *The Truth of Poetry: Tensions in Modern Poetry from Baudelaire to the 1960s*. London: Weidenfeld and Nicolson, 1969. [C.H.S. shows the internationalism that was a part of the experience of poets who went to war. However in spite of his intelligence and his criticism of Rupert Brooke, he remained bound by conventions of expression abandoned by his continental counterparts.]

Hopkins, Kenneth. *English Poetry: A Short History*. New York: J. B. Lippincott Co., 1962. [By 1916, both sides were sick of the war, but "they had not yet taken the further step of questioning its purpose." Julian Grenfell and C.H.S. might have spoken to this point had they not died in 1915. The work of both has within it "the potential of a message more realistic than Rupert Brooke's."]

Housman, Laurence, ed. *War Letters of Fallen Englishmen*. London: Victor Gollancz, Ltd., 1930. [Reprints the following letters: To Arthur Watts, 1 June 1915; To Arthur Watts, 16 June 1915; To His Father, 15 July 1915; To the Master of Marlborough, 4 August 1915; To Arthur Watts, 26 August 1915; To Arthur Watts, 2 October 1915.] Blunden, Edmund. "Review of *War Letters of Fallen Englishmen*." *Votive Tablets: Studies Chiefly Appreciative of English Authors and Books*. London: Cobden Sanderson, 1931. [Sorley's letter of July 15, 1915, "communicating with a wealth of original metaphor the normal sounds and sights of nightfall on the Flanders battlefield" is . . . "near the best of this kind of perpetuation achieved hitherto."]

Hussey, Maurice, ed. *Poetry of the First World War*. London: Longmans, Green and Co. Ltd., 1967. [C.H.S.'s poetry reveals "a swiftly maturing personality which possessed the highest potential greatness." Considerably younger than D. H. Lawrence, C.H.S. lacks his "colloquial freedom." Still, in "When You See Millions of the Mouthless Dead," one can note that although the rhetoric is romantic, "the heart is changing." Allowances must be made for technical immaturity, but in attitude several of his poems "strike independent ground."]

Isaacs, Abram. "Letter." *Nation*, 108 (April 19, 1919), 610; reprinted, *The Living Age*, 303 (Oct. 4, 1919), 43. [There are two Americas: one "fearless . . . in its quest for civil and religious freedom; . . . the other slavish, subservient" and "endangering the very life spirit of our republic by the intensity of its hatreds and hypocrisies." Both sides should read Sorley's "To Germany."]

Johnston, John Hubert. "Charles Sorley's 'Bright Promise.'" *West Virginia University Philological Papers*, 13 (Dec. 1961), 65-75. [Although C.H.S.'s "small body of verse can support no major revaluation of his place in literature . . . a brief examination of his attitudes and techniques indicates to what extent he might have excelled Siegfried Sassoon . . . and Wilfred Owen . . . in a comprehensive artistic evaluation of the effects of modern warfare on the human spirit." C.H.S. had an unusually perceptive mind which would have rejected Sassoon's "undisciplined realism" as well as Owen's "theme of pity" as inadequate for the tragic experience of modern warfare .

———. *The Poetry of World War I: A Study in the Evolution of Lyric and Narrative Form. Dissertation Abstracts*, 20 (1960), 4397-4398. *English Poetry of the First World War: A Study in the Evolution of Lyric and Narrative Form*. Princeton: Princeton University Press, 1964. ["Two or three of Sorley's poems rank with any others inspired by the conflict, and, as specimens of the early response, they display a grasp of reality altogether beyond the talents of Brooke, Grenfell, or Nichols." C.H.S.'s technique is "austere," indicating a sort of stoic attitude based on a recognition that "pity is irrelevant when its object is the victim of forces beyond human control or understanding." His point of view is essentially "detached" and "tragic."]

Jones, J. B. "Sorleiana." *The Swindon Review: A Local Miscellany of the Arts*, No.4 (Dec. 1948), 16-19. [After the destruction of the Four Mile Clumpstone by a British army tank on maneuvers, the author arranged for the protection of the Five Mile Stone and subsequently carved Sorley's initials on it as identifying marks.]

Kyle, William Galloway, ed. *Soldier Poets*. London: Erskine MacDonald, 1916. [Prints two poems not originally printed in Marlborough and Other Poems: *Faust, Part II*, ll. 6944-72, 6820-3, and the sonnet "Prometheus Vinctus Loquitur." C.H.S. "ingeniously" combined "the separate passages into a single piece."]

Leonard, Sterling Andrus, ed. *Poems of the War and the Peace*. New York: Harcourt, Brace and Co., 1921. [C.H.S.'s verse shows "beautiful promise," and, especially in "To Germany," it exhibits "fine and broad tolerance."]

Logue, Leona Whitworth. *Recent War Lyrics: A Study of War Concepts in Modern Lyrics*. New York: Grafton Press, 1928. [C.H.S. was a "promising young" poet who found time during the war to assert the fundamental brotherhood of Englishmen and Germans.]

Mackerness, E. D. "Charles Hamilton Sorley." *Die Neueren Sprachen*, N. S., 7 (July 1961), 330-334. [A generation "sated" by early Georgian poetry may have welcomed C.H.S.'s poetry because of its "unaffected freedom from artifice." Yet there are other reasons for sustaining a high estimate of his work. Unlike Brooke, Sorley was of a critical frame of mind, thus his poetry begins in a respectable "intellectual position." He entered the war with no illusions about its "splendor," and he could not create a "vision of 'the Enemy.'" More importantly, he "attempted to render the spiritual condition of those who were just beginning to live with the monstrosity of daily attack and counter-attack."]

Manley, John Matthews and Edith Rickert, comps. *Contemporary British Literature: Bibliographies and Study Outlines*. New York: Harcourt, Brace, and World, 1921. [Presents a brief biographical sketch of Sorley and suggestions for reading.]

Mee, Arthur. "The Poet of Life's Swift Radiant Morning." *1000 Heroes* (Issued in Weekly Parts), No. 13, pp. 607-610. [C.H.S. was noteworthy for his sincerity and frankness. He loved the Marlborough Downs and Marlborough College. His youthful paper on John Masefield "remains the most substantial and sustained evidence of his intellectual power."]

Mégroz, R. L. *Modern English Poetry: 1882-1932*. Strand: Ivor Nicholson and Watson, Ltd., 1933. [C.H.S. is one of those war poets who "would not or could not move themselves to write mainly war poetry during the years of horror."]

Moir, Guthrie. *The Suffolk Regiment*. London: Leo Cooper, Ltd., Famous Regiments Series, 1969. [A history of Sorley's regiment which notes Robert Graves's statement that C.H.S. was one of the three poets of importance to be killed in the First World War.]

Moore, T. Sturge. "Soldier Poets (V)." *The English Review*, 27 (Oct. 1918), 259-267; reprinted, "Sorley," Some Soldier Poets. London: Grant Richards, 1919; reprinted, Freeport, N. Y.: Books for Libraries Press, 1968. [C.H.S. was the youngest and possibly "the most hope-inspiring" of the war poets. Although his language is "poor and thin," it suggests "organic forms." The poet was "an unusually clear-eyed and affectionate rebel, who did not only feel that things were wrong, but could point them out with an unerring finger."]

Munro, John M., ed. *English Poetry in Transition, 1880-1920*. New York: Pegasus, 1968. [Had C.H.S. lived, he might have become an important modem poet. He maintained a "balanced" attitude toward the war, though he "was sensitive enough to react against the brutality."]

Murphy, C. C. R. *The History of the Suffolk Regiment 1914-1927*, Vol. 2. London: Hutchinson and Co., Ltd., 1928. [Recounts Sorley's service record from the date of his commission on Aug. 26, 1914 until his death on Oct. 13, 1915.]

Murry, John Middleton. "The Lost Legions." *The Athenaeum*, No. 4683 (Jan. 30, 1920), 136-138. [Sorley produced poems that are "among the most remarkable of those of the boy-poets killed in the war." His letters reveal little bitterness and an unusually keen critical intellect for a boy of nineteen.]

Nevinson, Margaret Wynne. "Some of Our Young War Poets." *The English Review*, 29 (Sept. 1919), 224-233; reprinted, *The Living Age,* 303 (Oct. 4, 1919), 40-45. [The English soldier-poets do not write "hymns of hate"; in fact they "seem to leave anger and bitterness to the civilian and the press." C.H.S.'s "To Germany" illustrates this observation.]

Nichols, Robert, ed. *Anthology of War Poetry*. London: Nicholson and Watson, 1943. [The preface is a discussion between the "Anthologist" and Julian Tennyson. The Anthologist asserts C.H.S. to have been "probably the most clear-sighted English poet killed" in the war. Sorley's criticism of Brooke's "sentimental attitude" toward the war shows the clarity of his insight. The Anthologist reports John Masefield's belief that C.H.S. "was potentially the greatest poet lost to us in that war, and that, had Sorley lived, he might have become our greatest dramatist since Shakespeare." The Anthologist agrees, but argues that Sorley would have been a dramatist of the stamp of Corneille.]

Obituary of Charles Hamilton Sorley. *The Marlburian* (Nov. 24, 1915). [C.H.S. was extraordinarily gifted, impressing his associates at Marlborough College with his "exuberant vigour of mind and body." Loving the wind and rain, he chose John Masefield and Richard Jefferies as favorite poets. To those who knew of "his admiration . . . for some things German, there is a tragedy in his death yet the greater."]

Osborn, Edward Bolland. "The Absolute Poet." *The New Elizabethans*. London: John Lane, The Bodley Head, 1919. [C.H S.'s. best poetic manner is characterized by the "precision" and "earnestness" of the Hellenic Greeks. No sentimentalist, he saw through "Pan-German" types and at the same time admired the Germans' lack of reserve and self-consciousness. His poetry reflects his Hellenism: it is "above and beyond the mannered subtleties of the Late-Victorian poets and men of letters .... His language is clear, reflecting Browning's zest for life and "Emily Brontë's eager undazzled gaze and scorn of excess verbiage."]

———. *The Muse in Arms: A Collection of War Poems, for the Most Part Written in the Field of Action, by Seamen, Soldiers, and Flying Men Who are Serving or Have Served, in the Great War*. New York: Frederick A. Stokes Co., 1917. [C.H.S.'s "To Germany" is an example of an attitude characteristic of the verse of English soldier-poets: "the complete absence of the note of hatred for a most hated enemy." The poem is sorrowful instead of angry.]

———. "Real War Poetry." *The Saturday Review*, 123 (March 3, 1917), 202-204; reprinted, *The Living Age*, 293 (April 14, 1917), 92-96. [The patriotism of the English soldier-poets transcends 'isms'; it can be "shadowed forth" only by the familiar characteristics of the countryside or by the "curious laws and quaint customs of schools and colleges. . . ." The "profoundly significant" poetry of C.H.S. reflects these similitudes.]

———. "Soldier Poets." The Living Age, 296 (Jan. 5, 1918), 48-52; originally printed in *Chambers Journal*. [The death of C.H.S. and other poets of "achievement" and "promise" is "a sad loss to English literature." English soldier-poets did not write a poetry of hate. It was the "offense, not the offenders," that they despised. Thus, C.H.S. could write "To Germany."]

Palmer, Herbert. "The Great War in Poetry." *Cornhill*, 157 (March 1938), 363-376. [Killed in the war, C.H.S. wrote little poetry directly applicable to the war. He was a poet of "great promise."]

———. "The Poetry of the Great War." *Post-Victorian Poetry*. London: J. M. Dent and Sons, 1938. [C.H.S. and Siegfried Sassoon gave voice to a feeling of "forgiveness to the enemy." Sorley was a poet of "great promise."]

Parsons, Ian McNaughten, ed. *Men Who March Away: Poems of the First World War*. New York: Viking Press, 1965. [The poets who died early in the war were more optimistic than the later soldier-poets and, generally speaking, employed "worn out modes." C.H.S.'s "All the Hills and Vales Along" characterizes the mood of "optimistic exhilaration" with which many persons greeted the beginning of the war. Yet this poem is "strangely ambivalent" and is "a technical triumph astonishing in a young man who was only twenty when he was killed."]

Parsons, Mary Prescott. "War and Peace." *The New Poetry: A Study Outline.* New York: The H. W. Wilson Company, 1922. ["To Germany" in *Marlborough and Other Poems* is recommended reading.]

Phillips, Charles. "Sursum Corda! —Some Notes on War Poetry." *Catholic World,* 106 (Feb. 1918), 606-617. [C.H.S. was one of several young poets killed in the war. *Marlborough and Other Poems* is a combination of fulfillment and promise. "All the Hills and Vales Along" is a "real achievement."]

Pinto, Vivian de Sola. "Trench Poets." *Crisis in English Poetry, 1880-1940.* London: Hutchinson's University Library, 1951. [C.H.S. is "the first poet of the war generation to explore the profounder meaning of the crisis .... " His poetry also presents a new attitude toward the war dead: death in action is too terrible for a cheaply emotional response. His attitudes anticipate those of Wilfred Owen.]

Press, John. "Charles Sorley." *A Review of English Literature,* 7 (April 1966), 43-60. [Critics who find C.H.S.'s poetry as "a stepping stone" from Brooke to Sassoon are mistaken. Sorley "was not disillusioned by his experience of fighting because he had no illusions to shed." His poems about war are the products of a mind that clearly perceived the nature of the conflict from its beginning. Sorley's principal weaknesses as a poet are "a conventionality of diction" and a lack of "strong personal rhythm." His strengths are "clarity of mind" and a "desire to follow the truth wherever it might lead." Had he lived he might have written a poetry of war closer to the requirements of W. B. Yeats than to the pity of Wilfred Owen.]

The Recorder. "A Bibliography of Modern Poetry, with Notes on Contemporary Poets." *The Chapbook: A Monthly Miscellany*, 2 (June 1920), 2·46. [For one with such a limited experience, C.H.S. showed "a remarkable maturity and depth of insight." Unlike other war poets, he did not achieve his effects by "bitter invective and pseudo-realistic descriptions of battlefields." The dominant qualities of his poetry are "restraint and dignity."]

Rickword, Edgell. "War and Poetry (1914-1918), Part 2: From Rhetoric to Realism." *Life and Letters Today,* 26 (July 1940), 26-35. [The "depth of disillusionment" reached in 1915 was sounded by C.H.S. in "When You See Millions of the

Mouthless Dead." In this sonnet, the "pretty fictions" are stripped away. The sonnet anticipates the "pity" of Wilfred Owen.]

Riding, Laura and Robert Graves. *A Survey of Modernist Poetry*. London: William Heineman Ltd., 1929. ["Of the war poets whose works were temporarily advertised by their death in action only three can be regretted: Sorley, Rosenberg, and Owen."]

Rittenhouse, Jessie B. "Poets Militant." *Bookman* (London), 47 (March 1918), 93-98. [The young soldier-poets "lift the cup of battle to their lips as if it were the Grail." C.H.S.'s volume "is full of the soldier's dedicated gladness. "]

Roberts, Michael, ed. *Faber Book of Modern Verse*. London: Faber and Faber, 1936. [C.H.S.'s poetry was not included because it does not contribute to the development of poetic technique.]

Routh, H. V. *English Literature and Ideas in the Twentieth Century*. London: Methuen and Co., 1948. [C.H.S. succeeded better than any of the other early war poets "in expressing the charm and gracefulness of his talent on a background of trench warfare."]

Sampson, George. *The Concise Cambridge History of English Literature*. Cambridge: Cambridge University Press, third edition (revised), 1970. [C.H.S. was one of the "best" of the poets killed in the war. The "simple patriotism of Rupert Brooke was answered" by a few of Sorley's poems.]

Scott-James, R. A. " *'Georgian' Poets," Fifty Years of English Literature, 1900- 1950*. London: Longmans, Green and Co., 1951. [It is impossible to determine what C.H.S. would have become. "His poetry ... is that of a boy writing with sensibility and fineness and a touching confidence in his nation's cause." He was killed before he had developed "an original style."]

"Soldier Poets." *The American Review of Reviews*, 58 (Nov. 1918), 554-556. [The story of Rupert Brooke is well-known in America, but there are many other deceased war poets whose stories are unknown. Such a poet is C.H.S.]

Stead, C. K. *The New Poetic: Yeats to Eliot*. London: Hutchinson University Library, 1964; Pelican Books, 1967. [C.H.S., like Sassoon and Owen, inherited " ... the liberal intellectual movement out of which had come the Georgian anthologies." They attacked the false attitudes toward war "with a true presentation of the facts."]

Strachan, R .H. *The Soul of Modern Poetry*. London: Hodder and Stoughton, 1924. [The appeal of modern war poetry is to "thought and imagination" instead of to the "glory of war." C. H. S. wrote "one of the most far-seeing and most courageous utterances" of the conflict in "To Germany." In "All the Hills and Vales Along," C.H.S. avoids the "self-consciousness of the poet, consecrating himself to sacrifice," which he had criticized as a fault in the poems of Rupert Brooke.]

Strong, L. A. G. "English Poetry Since Brooke." *Nineteenth Century*, 116 (Oct. 1934), 460-468; reprinted, *American Mercury*, 35 (May 1935), 56-62. [The "faltering course of English poetry from 1914-1930" is the result of the war. Besides killing such "actual poets as Owen, Sorley, Mackintosh," and an unknown number of "potential poets, it laid its mark heavily upon those whom it left alive."]

Swann, Thomas Burnett. *The Ungirt Runner: Charles Hamilton Sorley, Poet of World War I*. Hamden, CT.: Archon Books, 1965. [The only full-length critical biography of C.H.S., it leans heavily on Sorley's poems and letters for biographical materials. It was unfavorably reviewed in *Choice*, 2 (Jan. 1966), 774]

Swinnerton, Frank. *Background with Chorus: A Footnote to Changes in English Literary Fashion between 1901 and 1917*. London: Hutchinson and Co., Ltd., 1956. [C.H.S. was one of the group of early poets who composed "heroic songs." This sort of verse was quickly followed by a literature of "disenchantment."]

———. *The Georgian Scene: A Literary Panorama*. New York: Farrar and Rinehart, 1934; revised, *The Georgian Literary Scene: A Panorama*. London: William Heineman Ltd., 1935; further revised, London: Hutchinson and Co. Ltd., 1969. [C.H.S. was one of the early poets to say in print what they felt about the war. These poets were "duly read and celebrated"; however, the heroic note gave way to another note altogether.]

Tinker, Chauncey B. "British Poetry Under Stress of War." *Yale Review*, N.S.,9 (July 1920), 714-726. [At the outbreak of the war, "the old Victorian notes of thwarted search and wistful regret reappeared. . . . Yet there was too much of high spiritual adventure in the poet militant to permit him to rest content with negatives." C.H.S.'s best lyric, "Expectans Expectavi," is far from the mood of the Victorian age. Perhaps there is no poet "whose death is more grievously to be deplored than Sorley's." His poetic qualities are "largeness of phrase," "imaginative scope," and a "sense of unrealized power."]

Trotter, Jacqueline T., ed. *Valour and Vision: Poems of the War 1914-1918*. London: Longmans, Green and Co., 1920; enlarged, 1923. ["'When You See Millions of the Mouthless Dead' is illustrative of the "sterner note" taken by English war poets beginning in 1915.]

Untermeyer, Louis, ed. *Modern British Poetry*. New York: Harcourt, Brace, and World, 1962. [C.H.S. was "the most brilliant of the "younger poets." He saw through the sentimental attitudes of Rupert Brooke.]

Ward, A. C. "Charles Hamilton Sorley." *Longman Companion to Twentieth Century Literature*. London: Longman Group Ltd., 1970. [Incorrectly notes that C.H.S. was educated at Oxford and incorrectly notes that the biographical preface to the Letters (1919) was written by C.H.S.'s brother.]

Waugh, Arthur. "War Poetry (1914-1918)." *Tradition and Change: Studies in Contemporary Literature*. London: Chapman and Hall, 1919. [Many of the war poets draw on their days in school, "fighting old battles over again on field and in classroom." Thus emerges the public school soldier "bred on good literature and good sport," reading Homer in the trenches. Such a poet was C.H.S., "whose imagination seems to flood the squalid present with the heroism of the past."]

Weygandt, Cornelius. *The Time of Yeats: English Poetry of To-day Against an American Background*. New York: D. Appleton-Century Co., 1937. [It is too early to judge the endurance of poems by C.H.S. and the other war poets. Sorley's poetry has the mood of "homesickness" about it.]

Williams, George Guion. "British Poetry of Two World Wars." Rice Institute Pamphlet, 29 (Oct. 1942), 360-386. [C.H.S. was made a poet by the war. His "To Germany" reveals the British soldier-poet's lack of hatred for the enemy.]

Willson, St. J. B. Wynne. Letter to *Times Literary Supplement* (Oct. 28, 1915), 381. (C.H.S. ranks with Rupert Brooke "for promise." Sorley possessed "brilliant intellectual endowments."]

Reviews of Books by and About Sorley

Marlborough and Other Poems.

"The Fighting Poets." *The Morning Post* (June 23, 1916). ["Had he lived, the late Captain Charles Sorley would have held a high place among the Georgian poets." His poems are free from "clever insincerity and painted rhetoric.... With him thought must be unadorned, spirituality stark-naked; his style has the sad earnestness and vivid exactness which as Newman said, are characteristic of Greek poetry."]

Hicks, G. Dawes. "Charles Sorley's Poems." *Hibbert Journal*, 14 (April 1916), 659-661. [Although C.H.S. would not have published his poems without considerable revision, in their present form they exhibit more than promise. "Many of them strike a note of rare beauty and sweetness, and cannot fail to make their appeal to minds of varying temperaments." Throughout the book there is a spirit of healthy optimism, and only occasionally does the poet raise "the standard of revolt."]

"Killed in Action." *The Evening Standard and St. James's Gazette* (Jan. 27, 1916). [C.H.S. was not a great poet. "His early death reminds one of Rupert Brooke's." But there are other similarities. Although "Brooke reached a melody which Sorley did not aim at ... they seem to have thought, to have dreamed and hoped, even as occasionally they wrote, remarkably alike." Both men loved the English countryside. "Both went to Germany, and found a difficulty in breathing freely there. Both expressed their longing for home with humour. Neither was bound by any tradition of the gravity, the so-called dignity, of verse." C.H.S.'s sincerity is his most striking characteristic. He wrote what he felt and did not strive for "grand language."]

The Morning Post (Sept. 14, 1917). ["Sound judges are beginning to think that ... Charles Sorley's scant legacy of poetry — bleak, bright heroical stuff ... — is the witness to a poetical gift that will soon be upon us."]

"'Two Soldier Poets.'" *Times Literary Supplement* (Feb. 10, 1916), 66. [C.H.S. achieved more than "promise." His poems show "boyishness," "a little pompousness," and "an uncertain wit"; however, the qualities of his poetry are "gaiety, courage, and modest self-confidence."]

The Letters
"Charles Sorley." *The Cambridge Review* (June 4, 1920), 383-384. [The letters are interesting as documents which record "the reaction of German life and thought upon this gifted and clear-sighted boy. . . ." But in terms of their "form and style," "the continual criticism of literature," and "the vivid expression of a rich and radiant personality," they have a "lasting literary value."]

"A Knight-Errant." *Manchester Guardian* (Dec. 11, 1919). [Even if C.H.S. had never written poetry, this volume would have been "invaluable" as a document recording "the first mature impressions of a nature which was all vigour and radiance, a boy who may be said to have had a genius for truth." From the letters emerges "the portrait of a veritable knight-errant, one by whom the test of the war was accepted without a tremor, though nothing could have been farther from his nature than fighting. . . . His experience in Germany opened his mind to the German point of view."]

***English Poetry of the First World War*, by John Johnston.**
Bergonzi, Bernard. *The Listener*, 72 (July 30, 1964), 171. [Johnston is just "to the brilliantly talented Charles Sorley . . . whose letters reveal an extraordinarily mature critical intelligence. . . ."]

Burke, Fidelian. *Thought*, 40 (Summer 1965),295-297. [Johnston dismisses the early poets, C.H.S. among them, as essentially Georgian. These poets "had little experience of the war's sustained carnage [and] were preoccupied with the effect of the war on their personal lives."]

Davie, Donald. "In the Pity." *New Statesman*, 68 (Aug. 28, 1964), 282- 283. [Most of the war poets were amateurs, but without the work of such professionals as Brooke the value of their poems would diminish. C.H.S.'s "All the Hills and Vales Along" is one of the few early poems that "can bear up under our hindsight.]

Day, Douglas. *South Atlantic Quarterly*, 64 (Summer 1965),422-423. [C.H.S. was a complex, clear-sighted young man who perceived the truth of the war long before the later war poets.]

Fuller, Roy. *The London Magazine*, 4 (Sept. 1964), 95-96. [Johnston's book gives "proper credit to the intelligent Sorley ... ."]

King, Carlyle. "Poetry and War." *Canadian Forum* (Aug. 19(4), 120. [By "the standards of epic and heroic literature" which Johnston accepts, Sorley, Brooke, Grenfell, and Nichols are "quickly dismissed .... "]

Panichas, George A. *Modern Language Journal*, 49 (Feb. 1965), 118-119. [The coming of the war brought an increase in "self-contemplation" and a heightening of emotional sensibility. It is with C.H.S. "that undisciplined emotionalism and subjectivism were more sharply curtailed."]

Potter, Stephen. "The Plan of Attack." *Spectator* (July 31, 1964), 156. [C.H.S. is an example of the rushing into verse of a poet whose "power of creation" was "quickened" by the fear of early death.]

Rosenthal, M. L. *Victorian Studies*, 9 (March 1966), 279-282. [C.H.S. was a "brilliantly promising young Scotsman" who was killed in the war.]

Thomas, R. George. *The Review of English Studies*, N. S., 17 (Feb. 1966), 103-105. [Rosenberg is praised because, like C.H.S., "he evinces an ironic detachment from the mood of 'romantic self-contemplation'" which marks the Georgian attitude.]

Willingham, John R. *Library Journal*, 89 (April 1, 1964), 1611. [The early war poets — Brooke, Grenfell, Nichols, and Sorley — shared "a grandly abstract idealism."]

Heroes' Twilight, by Bernard Bergonzi.

"Arma Virumque: the Poetry of Three Wars." *Times Literary Supplement* (March 10, 1966), 186. [Bergonzi performs a "timely service" in restoring C.H.S. as one of the most interesting poets of his generation. Sorley was not deluded about the nature of the war. The "dualism" in his thought revealed by his attitudes toward death links him with Sassoon and Owen.]

Ascherson, Neal. "Intoxicated With War." *New York Review of Books*, 7 (Oct. 6, 1966), 19-20. [C.H.S. was "the detached, rather pro-German public schoolboy who had little patience with big talk about death." He was "subtle and thorough," avoiding a "surrender to direct pity and rage. . . ."]

Cohen, J. M. "The Earth is Hungry." *The Listener*, 74 (Nov. 11, 1965), 753-754. [C.H.S. and Ernest Stadler, a German poet killed at Ypres in 1914, rejected the "mood of unthinking patriotism." Sorley "had probably greater promise as a poet than any other British casualty of his generation." Although less farsighted than C.H.S., Stadler saw himself "whirled by the forces of nature to extinction" and saw the face of his brother mirrored by the faces of the dead enemy soldiers.]

Featherstone, Joseph. *New Republic*, 154 (Feb. 5, 1966), 21-24. [The Battle of the Somme in 1916 is the dividing line of the war. "After that, the poems of Brooke, Grenfell, and Sorley, the Georgians, have a wispy self-centered look." These writers form an obvious contrast with the later war poets.]

Gersh, Gabriel. *The Georgia Review*, 21 (Summer 1967), 278-280. [C.H.S. is the "most interesting poet of the early phase" of the war. His "sardonic, wary intelligence" is evident in both his poems and his "remarkable letters."]

Kleine, Don W. *College English*, 28 (Jan. 1967), 336. [Bergonzi separates the men from the boys. C.H.S. was a boy.]

Thorpe, Michael. *Leuende Talen*, 240 (June 1967), 413-414. [C.H.S. was a "level-headed poet" who recognized "the antagonists' mutual vices" and saw through "the insular patriot's flatulent postures .... "]

PROMETHEUS VINCTUS LOQUITUR[151]

Far from the farthest bounds of earth — a land
Where never yet hath foot of mortal trod,
Illimitable, pathless — here, a god
God-bound, god-tortured, god-consumed I stand.
All day the sun beats down upon the sand
    Scorching the listless air; and all the night
    The moon gleams cold with pale impassive light
Holding an icy sway — and still I stand!

And let me stand so and defy them all!
    The martyr's exultation leaps in me,
And I am joyous, joyous. He shall fall,
    And I, whom he hath trampled on, shall see
His utter desolation: great that fall
    From heaven's height to hell's iniquity!

C.H.S., 1911

---

[151] *Prometheus Vinctus Loquitur.* "Prometheus Bound, Speaks." The theme of Prometheus, bound to a rock by Zeus, attracted poets from Aeschylus to Shelley and beyond. Sorley, at age 16, can perhaps be forgiven for introducing a reference to Christian martyrdom into pagan myth. The poem strikes home, though, since Prometheus is more honored than Zeus as a figure of romantic defiance. Since the pagan "Hell" is merely cold, sombre Hades, the actual Hell Sorley may have in mind is the Hell of being unworshipped and unremembered. —BR

BIOGRAPHICAL NOTE (1919)

By JANETTA SMITH SORLEY

[The following biographical note is by the author's mother, written as the opening chapter of *The Letters of Charles Sorley*, published in 1919. Text in brackets added for clarification of names and other family details.]

CHARLES HAMILTON SORLEY was born on 19th May 1895, in 44 Don Street, Old Aberdeen, and was the elder twin son of William Ritchie Sorley then professor of moral philosophy in Aberdeen University. [The poet's brother was named Kenneth William]. On both sides he was of Lowland Scottish descent, his forbears having come, so far as is known, from the lands between the Tay and the Tweed. One grandfather, the Reverend William Sorley, was, as a young man, among the ministers of the Scottish Church who "came out" at the Disruption of 1843:[152] his humour, force of character, and keenness of mind made him a man of mark in his day in the life of the border country. The other grandfather, who was known and loved by Charlie, is George Smith, C.I.E., of Edinburgh, a journalist and man of letters, much of whose life was spent in India.

A year after the boys' birth their family moved to Powis House, a fine Adams mansion standing high above the Old Town and looking over the dream-like crown of King's College Chapel to the rim of the North Sea. It is a fine windy place and a good natural nursery for children ; the fields round the house were filled with beasts; and there is the exciting neighbourhood of a local railway station, which inspired the children to create imaginary kingdoms of their own "up the line," connected by a vast railway system one of whose rules was that all the officials must cross the line by the bridges only while passengers and others might do as they pleased.

At Powis the boys and their elder sister spent four happy years of normal and contented childhood, sometimes going

---

[152] *Disruption of 1843*. A schism within the Established Church of Scotland that pitted church independence against the State.

Charles and Kenneth Sorley, c. 1905

with their beloved nurse to her home by the North Sea, where they learned to plant potatoes or ranged the windy moors in search of lapwings' eggs, coming home full of barn-door wisdom and the life-histories of every creature on the farm. In 1900, when the boys were five years old, they came to live in Cambridge, "where the low streams run," as their father [William Ritchie Sorley] was appointed Knightbridge professor in the University. Until then and for some years after they were taught at home by their mother. Their education, besides the acquisition of an angular handwriting, consisted chiefly in singing and marching games in French and English, history stories and fairy stories, reading aloud from the Bible and the *Pilgrim's Progress*, but especially in learning by heart any amount of poetry — ballads and passages of Shakespeare, Walter Scott, Macaulay, and Blake. With "Once more unto the breach, dear friends," Sir Patrick Spens, or "Tiger, tiger, burning bright" humming in their heads, it was vaguely disappointing to be set down to Mrs Hemans[153] and Mary Howitt,[154] when they first went to school. It is sad to have to record that well-meant efforts to interest them in natural history failed completely, nor did they ever have much inclination to collect stamps, play with bottles, or maim themselves with tools. But they were eager to write down whatever came into their heads or seemed to them worth remembering and telling about. When they were about ten, their sister [Jean] had a hand in the inevitable school magazine for which she demanded contributions. Among other efforts Charlie gave her the following verses :

---

[153] *Mrs. Hemans.* Felicia Dorothea Browne Hemans (1793-1835), prolific author of historical, biblical, narrative and topical poems.
[154] Mary Howitt (1799-1800), poet and author of more than 180 books, many written expressly for children, including *Tales in Prose for the Young* (1839) and the series *Mary Howitt's Illustrated Library for the Young.* She also translated the fairy tales of Hans Christian Andersen into English.

THE TEMPEST

The tempest is coming,
   The sky is so dark,
The bee has stopped humming
   And down flies the lark.

The clouds are all uttering
   Strange words in the sky;
They are growling and muttering
   As if they would die.

Some forked lightning passes
   And lights up the place,
The plains and the grasses,
   A glorious space.

It is like a story
   The light in the sky:
A moment of glory
   And then it will die.

The rain is beginning,
   The sky is so dark,
The bird has stopped singing
   And down flies the lark.

    The beginning of school-life, as a day-boy at the King's College Choir School, meant nothing but satisfaction and happy anticipation to Charlie. He always wanted to grow up, and this was a stage farther on. Each new experience — whether game or book or place or human being — came as an adventure to him; he always criticized eagerly, but he reaped and remembered only the best — nothing else counted. "No, I haven't got a pain, but I can't help it when I think of the future," was his explanation when he was found crying in bed, with his head far under the clothes, after he had heard that scarlet fever would separate him for six long weeks from his brother and from school. This was an almost solitary instance of complaint or depression. Whatever disappointments, apprehensions, or sense of failure he ever had afterwards, he kept to himself and met his adventures — especially the greatest of all, in August 1914 with a happy readiness and humour that gave a sense of comfort and assurance to those about him. "There goes Charlie, aye bright and brave," as our old Yorkshire hostess said at the end of a holiday. At the same time he had a quick understanding of what failure, or weakness, or limitation means for other people and his sympathy was active — even to the extent of leading him on one occasion to deplore his own easy lot: "I often feel terribly unworthy and untried in that life has given me no troubles or difficulties at home, such as alone strengthen a man," he wrote to a friend in 1915. Everybody and everything interested and had a claim on him. He knew that life had been good to him, and by instinct he gave back all he could.

In the choice of a public school Charlie was a pioneer, as his family had no previous experience or tradition to guide them. He settled the question for himself by gaining an open scholarship at Marlborough College, where he went in the autumn of 1908. The one drawback to this adventure was the separation from his brother, who was sent to another school because even the wisest of men and schoolmasters do not seem able to refrain from making comparisons; and it is fairer for a boy to be on his own. The boys were alike in the deep love and understanding they had for each other; but they had great independence of ideas and outlook and were for twins remarkably different in nature and appearance. They looked forward to being together at the University; and meanwhile there were the vacations which, in summer, were usually passed either at a Yorkshire inn where the moors approach the sea, or else in one or other of the home-places Selkirk, Dunbar, or Aberdeen. Once we went with bicycles to France, and rode about the coast of Normandy and the land by the Seine. Charlie's comment (it was his first time abroad) was that it was the rottenest country he had ever seen and the finest holiday he had ever had. We had the habit besides of going to Marlborough every summer — not for Speech Day, which he did not recommend, but earlier when the fern and beeches are fresh in the forest "and the downs are dimpling green." Once, on an afternoon of gusty rain, when we had struggled up a steep red road and were about to cross over to the downs, we came suddenly on a field covered with great white flints. "What a lot of stones, how hopeless it looks!" said one of us. But Charlie, who generally responded readily, said not a word; he only stared at the field as if he saw something written on it,[155] and then we all went on in silence.

He was thirteen when he entered Marlborough, and at first the school absorbed him completely. He had a period of hero-worship, very little qualified by criticism, for its demigods among the boys and masters; he abounded in the mysteries of its etiquette and slang; and he would pore by the hour over the blue School List, declaring that he knew by headmark most of the boys in it which may very well have been the case, as he had a quick memory for names and faces. His enthusiasms were always breaking forth in brilliant generalizations, which were as often cheerfully and relentlessly shelved. So at this time he was certain that there was nothing to beat the public school system: it was the finest in the world.

In January 1910 he and his friend Arthur Bethune-Baker entered one of the senior houses in college C House, the oldest and most beautiful of the buildings, and the home of the Adderley Library, which became for him a great resource and pleasure. In the following November Arthur died at school after a few days' illness. At the time Charlie took it very quietly, but it is certain that what had been achieved in that short life became a part of him which was never forgotten or left behind.

His attitude towards the school, though essentially loyal and filial, developed in breadth and humour as he found freedom and read and thought for himself. On one of the family visits to Marlborough he asked, with subdued excitement, whether we had seen *The Widow in the Bye Street*.[156] The reply was that we had but that it had been chained up from the youth of the flock. To which he answered, supremely scornful, "We take *The English Review* in the Sixth; and, anyway, I've bought a copy and am lending it to people."

---

[155] See Sorley's poem, "Stones."
[156] *Widow in the Bye Street*. John Masefield's shocking 1912 novel in verse, with depictions of the sex lives of the lower classes.

He took his share eagerly in the occupations and interests of the school, especially football and the O.T.C. But what he liked best was to tramp or run over the surrounding country. No one more enjoyed and valued his friends, or more willingly took and gave the best of company ; yet when he went for long walks, or for runs in shorts and jersey, over the downs, he chose to be alone. In July 1911 he bicycled from Marlborough to Cambridge in a day; but that passion soon passed ; and in the spring of 1912 he walked home, taking four days to the hundred miles or so of distance. It was stipulated that he should spend the nights in a bed under cover, and not under hedge or haystack as he proposed; but there are evidences that the condition — if there was one — was not taken too seriously by him. Part of his way lay along the bank of the canal by Hungerford; here he found the dead straight line of the tow-path so unbearable that, to keep going at all, he had to repeat aloud the thirty-fifth chapter of *Isaiah*, which he had just learned as an imposition. He gaily told his first teacher that it was the only portion of the Bible which he could remember by heart. In September 1913, in returning for what was to be his last term at school, he left the train at Fenny Stratford and had a three days' walk to Marlborough.

In December 1913 he gained a scholarship at University College, Oxford. In ordinary course he should have remained at Marlborough for the rest of the school-year till July 1914. But, after some discussion with the Marlborough authorities, his father decided to give him a short time abroad as a break between the grooves of public school and university. There is no doubt that the home of his heart was the Marlborough country, and it cost him something to give up the last six months there. But he left himself in the hands of of "the gods who made a pother o'er his head" and agreed to the plan with his usual happy reasonableness.

He had always kept up the habit of writing down what was in his mind. When he was a small boy this took the form of long screeds of heroic verse after the model of Scott or Macaulay. Later he indulged in stories of the "shocker" sort, which he used to tell in the dormitory at night as the works of one Jonathan Armstrong. As he grew older he became more and more reserved about his writing. Though his family knew vaguely of his connection with the school magazine, *The Marlburian*, he never saw fit to enlighten them on the subject. He would sometimes mention, however, in his letters, when he made a speech at the Debating Society, or read a paper to the Junior Literary Society started largely on his account, when he was in the Lower Sixth, by one of the junior masters — or to the senior society, to which he was admitted on promotion to the Upper Sixth. Before he left for Germany he was asked to mark his articles and verses in *The Marlburian* for preservation among the family archives and because his mother had an idea that something was "going on." At the time he did not respond to this badgering; but some weeks later he sent a batch of verses to her. This he continued to do regularly, generally for a birthday, till June 1915 when the last lot, "Two Sonnets," were sent from France. A few days before these arrived it was suggested to him that a slim volume should be published "for fun" and to relieve the tedium of the trenches. But he would have none of it: "for three years or the duration of the war, let be." He was equally discouraging when asked for a "gallery" letter for the private record of the daily life and doings of his battalion in France. His sense about such things was soldierly, and he disliked and dreaded anything in the way of advertisement or pose.

On the 20th January 1914 he went to Schwerin in Mecklenburg where, in the house of a lawyer [Dr. Karl Beutin] and his wife, he found friends and conditions of the happiest and most entertaining kind. After he had got some hold of the language he moved at the end of April to Jena as a student of the University. There he realised a different world. Schwerin in 1914 was a place where people still said grace before meat, and meant it. In Jena they were more knowing. Both were amazingly young. Following their merciless family custom, his parents visited him in June and made with him a little tour in Thuringia, which closed with a week-end at Jena. On the Saturday night he took us through a square which was full of students both men and women seated at tables drinking and singing under flaring lights. Their singing was beautiful; their faces were mostly stupid and, in the case of recent duellists, revolting. The next day, as we went up towards a hill on the outskirts of the town, we met many of them again both Korpsstudenten and Wandervögel all in ridiculous clothes and with self-conscious looks which suggested pantomime. As we sat under the scanty shade of some scrubby trees, looking down on Jena shimmering in "the laden heat," and talking of its strange inhabitants, Charlie said dreamily, "I can't make out those fellows; they are always gassing about Goethe and Schiller; I think they're just hypocrites. But they must have some grit; for, though they do nothing at all their first two years but drink and fight and folly, yet they pull themselves together in their third year and manage to get through their exams." The following day, in the University, we were shown the fresco of the students of 1813 marching away to war.

In the end of July he reluctantly turned his steps homeward. He had planned a week's walking tour with a friend [Hopper] in the Moselle valley ; thence he was to dash across Germany to Berlin, then join his brother [who had taken his place for German language lessons with the Beutins] at Schwerin and return with him a few days afterwards. The latter part of the programme was not carried out. On Sunday, 2nd August, he and his friend were arrested at Trier, and kept in separate cells for the rest of the day. One damning circumstance was that they had no hats, though Charlie gravely assured the officers who examined them that such was the habit of "the best people" in England. For him the long hours of that day were beguiled by the cheerful conversation of a soldier- prisoner in the next cell, who hailed him cautiously through a knot-hole in the wooden partition. They did their best for one another during the day, muttering through the hole in the wall, always mindful of the sentry in the corridor. The two tourists were released the same night, with permission and orders to leave the country. Charlie returned through Belgium, with little idea that he was making for the storm-centre. As his train passed through Liège, in the early afternoon of Monday, he roused himself from sleep to have a look at the place, but noticed nothing peculiar except the "Waterloo top-hats" of the soldiers. At Brussels and Antwerp, however, he had many difficulties till he succeeded in getting a passage on a vessel chartered by the British consul. He reached home on the evening of August 6th, still hatless and with little in his rucksack but a pair of sandals and a Jena beer-jug. [His brother Kenneth had boarded a train for the English channel on August 1 and made it home safely.]

The next morning he applied to the University Board of Military Studies for a commission in the Army, and his application was transmitted to the War Office. Then followed a period of irksome delay during which he went to Oxford and made another application there. He was just about to enlist as a private, which he always said was the really heroic thing to do, when he saw his name in the *Gazette* as second lieutenant in the seventh battalion — the first of the new "service" battalions — of the Suffolk Regiment. That day he had orders to join a training camp at Churn on the Berkshire downs — "first cousins to the Wiltshire downs," as he called them. In the third week of September he joined his battalion at Shorncliffe above Folkestone. Again he was happy in his fate. He quickly realised the great history and traditions of the regiment — the "Old Dozen" — and made friends among the officers and men. We visited him for a week-end in February 1915 while he was doing a musketry course at Hythe, which he thoroughly enjoyed. During a stormy walk on The Leas he stopped suddenly and pointed across to Shorncliffe. "That's where Napoleon was beaten," he said, "at Sir John Moore's musketry school"; and then, sweeping his hand down seaward, "and that's where the Kaiser will be beaten at Hythe."

In the end of May the battalion was sent to France at last. Charlie was then lieutenant; in August he was gazetted captain; in September there was a prospect of leave. His service during these months was chiefly in the trenches round Ploegsteert. After the opening of the Battle of Loos the battalion was moved south to take part in the offensive. In the night of 12th-13th October it took over front-line trenches in readiness for the morrow's attack; and he fell on the afternoon of the 13th, shot in the head by a sniper, as he led his company at the "hair-pin" trench near Hulluch.

SORLEY IN TRAINING

Shorncliffe, 25 January 1915
To A. E HUTCHINSON

How are you getting on? I can imagine it is not quite heaven. But neither is this. Heaven will have to wait until the war's over. It is the most asphyxiating work after the first fine glow of seeing people twice your age and size obey and salute you has passed off, as it does after a fortnight. The only thing is that the pay is good. The rest, as you are probably finding already, is complete stagnation among a mass of straps and sleeping-bags and water-bottles. War in England only means putting all the men of "military age" in England into a state of routinal coma, preparatory to getting them killed. You are being given six months to become conventional : your peace thus made with God, you will be sent out and killed. At least, if you aren't killed, you'll come back so unfitted for any other job that you'll have to stay in the Army. I should like so much to kill whoever was primarily responsible for the war. The alarming sameness with which day passes day until this unnatural state of affairs is over is worse than any so-called atrocities; for people enjoy grief, the only unbearable thing is dullness.

I have started to read again, having read nothing all the closing months of last year. I have discovered a man called D. H. Lawrence who knows the way to write, and I still stick to Hardy: to whom I never managed to convert you.

We talk of going out in March. I am positively looking forward to that event, not in the brave British drummer-boy spirit, of course, but as a relief from this boredom (part of which, by the way, is caused through Philpott having been away the last three weeks in hospital).

We don't seem to be winning, do we? It looks like an affair of years. If so, pray God for a nice little bullet wound (tidy and clean) in the shoulder. That's the place.

Sorry I haven't more to write nor had Lot's wife when she was half through being turned into salt; nor will you in three months' time.

CONCERNING RUPERT BROOKE

To MRS. SORLEY
Aldershot, 28 April 1915

I saw Rupert Brooke's death in *The Morning Post*. *The Morning Post*, which has always hitherto disapproved of him, is now loud in his praises because he has conformed to their stupid axiom of literary criticism that the only stuff of poetry is violent physical experience, by dying on active service. I think Brooke's earlier poems — especially notably "The Fish" and "Grantchester," which you can find in *Georgian Poetry* — are his best. That last sonnet-sequence of his, of which you sent me the review in the *Times Lit. Sup.*, and which has been so praised, I find (with the exception of that beginning "These hearts were woven of human joys and cares, Washed marvellously with sorrow" which is not about himself) overpraised. He is far too obsessed with his own sacrifice, regarding the going to war of himself (and others) as a highly intense, remarkable and sacrificial exploit, whereas it is merely the conduct demanded of him (and others) by the turn of circumstances, where non-compliance with this demand would have made life intolerable. It was not that "they" gave up anything of that list he gives in one sonnet: but that the essence of these things had been endangered by circumstances over which he had no control, and he must fight to recapture them. He has clothed his attitude in fine words: but he has taken the sentimental attitude.

Kenneth and I had the most delightful week-end. In spite of the rather dismal atmosphere of an empty Oriel, in which I should not like to remain more than two months at a time, we filled up the time most excellently. The night before, I went to town to see *Macbeth* at the Old Vic. — for they speak their lines clearly at the Vic., and *Macbeth* has more beautiful poetry in it than any other tragedy — and sat next to my anarchist theosophical friend in green, whose acquaintance I made eighteen months ago in the gallery of the Kingsway at *The Great Adventure*. I was eating chocolate almonds, of which

I had the wit to remember he had expressed himself as very fond.

I enclose my occasional budget [of poems]. You will notice that most of what I have written is as hurried and angular as the hand-writing: written out at different times and dirty with my pocket: but I have had no time for the final touch nor seem likely to have for some time, and so send them as they are. Nor have I had the time to think out (as I usually do) a rigorous selection, as fit for other eyes. So these are my explanations of the fall in quality. I like "Le Revenant" best, being very interested in the previous and future experience of the character concerned: but it sadly needs the file. You will also find the last of my Marlborough poems called "Lost" written in sideways on the foolscap.

CHARLES SORLEY AT THE FRONT

An account, written by a brother-officer, of a bombing expedition made on one of the last nights of July 1915.

"We were holding trenches just to the south of Ploegsteert wood. D Coy were on the left of the Battalion, about 100 yards from the Germans. That opposite C.'s platoon was, I think, the most interesting part of our line, as the Germans were working on it from the day we took over till the day we left. They seemed to be making a redoubt of some kind, and, as those were the days when shells were scarce, we couldn't ask the gunners to blow it up. . . . C. knew the ground in front of this better than anyone in the company: where the ditches and disused saps ran; where the different shell-holes lay; where the beetroot met the clover, and where the clover ended in a strip of long thin grass up to the enemy's wire. C. had been out crawling often before, just for the fun of the thing. . . .It was all planned out cleverly beforehand: C. and three other bombers to crawl up to within bombing distance, he leading and directing the show; four riflemen were to come up on the flank and cover their retirement. . . . It was a dark night and everything went off splendidly up to the point when the bombs were to be thrown. . . . The pins had all been taken out and the second signal was just being passed when the third bomber dropped his infernal machine. I think the others heard it thud and tried to get clear; at any rate he was stupid enough to fumble about in the long wet grass in an attempt to find it. There was a dreadful five seconds' suspense: then the thing exploded right under him.

In the confusion C. and one of the other men managed to throw their bombs, and that and the fire of the riflemen, who opened up a steady burst immediately, saved the party somewhat. C. crawled to the man who had dropped his bomb and dragged him into the shell-hole. . . .The shell-hole was his salvation. They had only just got into it when the Germans swept the ground with an absolute hail of rifle and machine-gun fire and lit up all around with Very lights[157]. . . . When

---

[157] *Very lights*. Flares fired from a pistol.

the Germans had quieted down a bit, some more men came out and helped to get the wounded in. The one with C. was in a very bad way and died soon after. C. said every bone in the upper part of his body must have been broken — it was like carrying a piece of living pulp — and he never forgot the curious inarticulate cry of the man as he picked him up...

"Next morning, a brilliant July day, I went round to pick up Intelligence and met C. on trench patrol. He had just come from breakfasting and was dressed in summer get-up; gum boots, breeches, shirt-sleeves, sambrown[158] belt and pistol. He had a bandage round his head, but only a very slight scratch from a fragment of bomb. He was walking along, reading from his German pocket edition of *Faust*. He told me the whole story of the raid: rather sorry that his plans had been let down just when they might have been so successful; but he took it all in his happy careless fashion."

---

[158] *Sambrown*. The Sam Browne belt, worn by officers, is a leather belt with a supporting strap that goes over one shoulder.

HIS LAST LETTER HOME

To PROF. SORLEY
5 October 1915

Many thanks for the letters which arrived with the rations this morning. We are now embarked on a very different kind of life; whether one considers it preferable or otherwise to the previous, depending on one's mood. It is going to be a very slow business, but I hope a steady one. There is absolutely no doubt that the Bosch is now on his way home, though it is a long way and he will have many halts by the wayside. That "the war may end any year now" is the latest joke, which sums up the situation....

You will have seen that we have suffered by the loss of our chief: also that our battalion has lost its finest officer otherwise commissioned ranks have been extraordinarily lucky. For the present, rain and dirt and damp cold. O for a bath! Much love to all.

BIBLIOGRAPHY

Coones, Paul & John Patten. *The Penguin Guide to the Landscape of England and Wales*. 1986. Harmondsworth, Middlesex: Penguin.

von Goethe, Johann Wolfgang. *Faust, I & II*. Charles E. Passage, trans. 1965. Indianapolis: Bobbs-Merrill Educational Publishing. [I should very much have preferred to recommend the superb Walter Kaufmann translation of 1961, but Kaufmann omits all the material relating to Helen of Troy. Passage, like the 19th century Faust translator Bayard Taylor, presents all of *Faust* in the meters employed in the German original.)

Graves, Robert. *Fairies and Fusiliers*. (1917). New York: Alfred A. Knopf.

Graves, Robert. *Good-Bye to All That*. (1929) Revised ed. 1998. Anchor Books.

Heath, Frank R. *Wiltshire*. (1911). 4th ed., 1919. London: Methuen & Co., Ltd. [Includes a chapter on Marlborough with its Roman and pre-history as understood in Sorley's time.]

Hogg, A.H.A. *A Guide to the Hill-Forts of Britain*. 1984. London: Paladin (Granada).

Homer. *The Odyssey*. A.T. Murray, trans. 1919. London: William Heineman Ltd.

Jefferies, Richard. *Wild Life in a Southern County*. (1848). 1881. London: Smith, Elder & Co.

———. *An English Village: A New Edition of 'Wild Life in a Southern County'* 1903. Boston: Little, Brown & Co. [Printed at Cambridge, with photographs of Wiltshire by Clifton Johnson.]

Jenkins, Jennifer. "The Berkshire & Marlborough Downs," in *The English Landscape*. 2000. New York: Viking Studio. 165-170.

Kyle, William Galloway, ed. *Soldier Poets*. 1916. London: Erskine MacDonald. [Includes Sorley's *Faust* translation and his sonnet, "Prometheus Vincit Loquitur."]

Nieragden, Göran. "Charles Sorley's 'Unenthusiastic Patriotism'". *Focus on Robert Graves and His Contemporaries*. 2:2 (1994) 31-34.

Pindar. *The Odes of Pindar, Including the Principal Fragments*. John Sandys, trans. (1915, rev. 1937) Cambridge, MA: Harvard University Press.

Powell, Anne. "Such is Thomas Hardy!" *The Thomas Hardy Journal* 4:3 (1988) 48-56. [Details about Sorley's love for Thomas Hardy, and his readings and studies in Germany.]

Sorley, Charles Hamilton. *Marlborough and Other Poems.* (1916). W.R. Sorley, ed. London: Cambridge University Press. [First edition Jan 1916; second edition Feb 1916; reprinted Feb, April and May 1916; third edition Nov 1916; fourth edition 1919, fifth edition 1922; "Miscellany" edition 1932; reprinted 1932.]

———. *Letters from Germany.* W.R. Sorley, ed. 1916. London: Cambridge University Press. [Privately printed.]

———. *The Letters of Charles Sorley, with a Chapter of Biography.* W.R. Sorley, ed. 1919. London: Cambridge University Press.

Spurgeon, C.H. *The Peculiar Sleep of the Beloved*, 1855. London: New Park Street.

Swann, Thomas Burnett. *The Ungirt Runner: Charles Hamilton Sorley, Poet of World War I.* 1965. Hamden, CT: Archon Books.

Uffelman, Larry K. "Charles Hamilton Sorley: An Annotated Checklist." *The Serif.* 10:4 (1973) 3-17.

Watts, Isaac. "Awake, our souls! Away our tears." No 672, 3 in John Wesley. *A Collection of Hymns for the Use of the People Called Methodists.* 1875.

Wells. Colin. *The Roman Empire.* 2nd ed. 1992. Cambridge: Harvard University Press.

Willoughby, L.A. "Three English Poets in Expressionist Berlin." *German Life and Letters.* 45:4 (1992) 301-22. [Details Sorley's brief visit to Berlin, and his acquaintance with German poetry.]

ABOUT THIS BOOK

This book was completely reset from the 1932 edition using Century Schoolbook type. The original Century design was executed for metal type by Linn Boyd Benton in 1894. The typeface was originally commissioned by Theodore DeVinne for his *Century Magazine*. During the 20th century, a number of typefaces based on Century became a standard for textbooks and primers because of the letterforms' high legibility.

Headlines are set in Rockwell. This typeface was introduced by the Inland Type Foundry in 1910 as Litho Antique. Morris Fuller Benton (son of the designer of the Century type family) cut several new variants of the font for American Type Founders in the 1920s.

Typography, proofreading and editing were done by Tim Terhaar at The Poet's Press.

Photographs of the Wiltshire landscape are by Clifton Johnson, from the 1903 edition of Richard Jefferies' *Wild Life in a Southern County*.

The cover photo depicts British troops marching into poison gas at the Battle of Loos.